Praise for Lost and Found

"Carol offers us a heartfelt, engaging story of one woman's courageous endeavor to find her authentic life. She reminds us that connecting and reconnecting to our core values is a key to rediscovering our lost self. Reading "Lost and Found" will inspire you to embark on the inner journey of recommitting to the deeper truth of your heart."

— Mary Elizabeth Lynch, J.D., Co-Founder and President of the Personal Transformation and Courage Institute

"This is the heart-opening story of Carol deLaski's growth and healing through her relationship with God and the love and beauty that came to flow into her life and through her. Both personal and universal, this is a wise and deeply hopeful book. Carol teaches and inspires me."

— James S. Gordon, MD, author of *Unstuck: Your Guide to the Seven-Stage Journey Out of Depression*; Founder and Director of The Center for Mind-Body Medicine

"Carol has written a warm, honest, and inspiring book that will surely serve as an encouragement and guide to others seeking love and faith in their own lives. Drawing insightfully and candidly on her own personal experiences she shares a journey seeking meaning and wholeness that learns from the failures and builds on the gifts that come her way. The result is a testimony to the way in which love in relationships is intertwined with the love of God. Many will enjoy and profit from taking this journey with her."

— Bruce C. Birch, author, Dean and Professor of Biblical Theology, Wesley Theological Seminary, Washington, DC

"Carol is a gifted leadership coach whose thought-provoking and enjoyable book is a great springboard for those seeking love and faith."

— Bruce D. Schneider, author of *Energy Leadership*; and Founder of the Institute for Professional Excellence in Coaching (iPEC)

Lost & Found

Dear Paula + Bob,

You are both treasures.

Ich liebe dich,

Carl

April 2014

Published by CdL Publishing
Frederick, MD

For more information about this product contact www.CaroldeLaski.com

Printed in the United States of America

First Trade Edition: 2014

ISBN 978-0-9911196-0-8
Self-help – Personal growth – Spiritual development – Life Coaching

For my mother, Nancy,
who taught me how to love and be loved.

Mom, you inspire me with your sense of adventure, your inquisitive mind, and your dedicated service to others. I am so grateful to be your daughter and to have you as one of my very best friends.

Dear Reader,

Journeys of faith evolve through subtle yet meaningful decisions.

Seeds of faith are scattered throughout many of our lives. As those seeds take root and develop, each of us chooses the word or words that we are most comfortable with to describe a force greater than ourselves—a force grounded in compassion and love. Throughout this book I use the word "God" and the masculine pronoun to identify this greater consciousness. The purpose of sharing my story, however, is to inspire you to discover new insights about your own faith. Therefore, as you read this book I encourage you to use the words that are most familiar and comfortable for you when referring to a universal Higher Being.

Relationships are the fertile ground upon which the seeds of love grow.

In writing about the lost times of my life, it is important for me to note that the people who were part of my suffering were also catalysts for my growth. I would not be the woman I am today without those experiences, and for that I am grateful. I continue to be amazed at the depth and complexity of the human heart and our ability to forgive, heal, and grow. To ensure privacy I have changed some of the names in my story.

Respectfully,

Carol

Contents

Part III: Found

Foreward:
The Lost and Found Box

Have you ever set out to find something you lost? If I misplace a thing of value, I search high and low for it; mentally and physically retracing my steps until I find it again. Although I delight in the rediscovery, I sometimes chide myself for having been so thoughtless as to have mislaid it in the first place. I can be especially hard on myself if the item has been right in front of me all along. How many of us have searched for a pair of eyeglasses only to realize that they are on top of our heads or for keys that are still in the ignition?

I have noticed that there is a direct correlation between the value of something and how hard I search for it. I need my eyeglasses and keys to function on a daily basis. Misplaced items of lesser value, however, can remain lost for quite some time before I happen upon them and express delight in finding them once more.

Many years ago, my mother worked as a secretary at a private middle school for girls. Having raised six children, she was well suited for this position, as it required her to juggle multiple duties at the same time. Not only did she type and mimeograph huge amounts of paperwork, she also attended to the needs of the dramatic and often disorganized students who paraded through her office in search of guidance and encouragement. My mother would patiently address their questions while answering the phone and completing other duties assigned to her.

Middle-school girls are a precious yet somewhat challenging population. As they struggle to find themselves, they frequently succumb to comparisons—whether to a model on the cover of a magazine, a pop culture idol, or one of their peers. As a grown woman, I vividly remember the angst of my preteen years, and I have always admired my mother for having been such a steady and reassuring presence for these girls.

One thing that struck me during my mom's 15-year tenure at the school was the Lost and Found box located in the main office. All mislaid items collected throughout the school would end up in that receptacle, and the contents accumulated as the year progressed. In June, everything would be removed from the box and displayed in a final attempt to reunite items with their rightful owners. Anything that wasn't claimed was then offered to the staff. The students often didn't realize the value of the items they had lost, and it was not unusual for some very nice things to be up for grabs. One year, I became the proud owner of a high-quality down sleeping bag that was part of the end-of-the-year leftovers. I was surprised that the owner hadn't retrieved it and felt lucky to have received it for free.

How often are we like these children, underestimating the value of something that we have lost in our lives and then neglected to reclaim it? This can happen in various aspects of life, but the area of particular interest to me is the loss of our spiritual selves. There have been times in my life when I didn't value my connection with a spiritual presence. I didn't think it was a priority and instead chose to chase after other things that I thought would bring me satisfaction and pleasure. I have learned, however, through some challenging life experiences, that there is nothing more important than my relationship with a Higher Being. It is now the source of my deepest contentment and fulfillment; it is the treasure of my soul.

In this book, I will share some of my experiences of being lost and the steps that led me to find a deep and lasting faith. We each have a unique life story to tell. It is through the sharing of our stories that we realize we have experiences in common with one another and know that we are not alone. There is great comfort in creating a bond around problems solved, challenges overcome, and rich lessons that have been learned. As you read, I hope that you will consider your own lost and found experiences.

What have you lost?

What have you already found?

What are you hoping to find?

What are you willing to change in order to obtain a greater sense of peace and contentment?

No matter how lost you have been, or currently are, the answers you seek lie within you. My hope is that you will gain new insights about yourself as you join me on this journey.

Introduction:
Zipping into Trust

"Are you ready?" the zip line instructor asked. I found myself strapped in a harness equipped with huge metal cords and carabineers that suspended me from an industrial-sized cable somewhere above my head. My toes danced on the wooden platform below me and butterflies danced in my stomach, as the strong arm of the instructor steadied my swaying body. I looked out ahead at the zip line course, which sloped down across the lake far below, and then rose up again over the land on the opposite side. Although I mainly felt the thrill of anticipatory excitement, there were some anxious thoughts swirling inside my helmeted head. *What if something goes wrong?* I asked myself, even though I knew I wasn't willing to turn back. As one of the leaders of a women's weekend retreat, I was the last participant to experience the zip line ride. The rest of the women were now gathered at the other end of the line, ready to receive me.

I had just witnessed my 80-year-old mother run the course. While I implicitly trusted the instructor and the equipment, I whispered a heartfelt prayer for Mom as she courageously stepped off the platform and went zipping across the lake. I have to admit that it was not an entirely selfless prayer; I have five siblings and I couldn't help thinking, *Dear God, please keep Mom safe. They will just kill me if anything happens to her!* I felt a sense of relief as Mom made it safely to the other end of the line. She was met with cheers as several of the 30 women gathered there caught her in their arms and congratulated her. My mother is an amazing person, and as she bravely overcame her fears that day, she inspired so many others to live life fully, regardless of their age.

Now, it was my turn. With a deep breath I gave a nod to the instructor who then released his hold on me. I moved to the edge of the platform, stepped off into thin air, and began the thrill of the ride. Feeling the initial free fall, and then the reassuring bounce of the cable as it held my weight, I sped forward on a fast descent toward the lake. The warm wind blew against my face, and the cable emitted a zipping sound above my head. The water seemed to be fast approaching and I prayed that I would not end up in it. *What's the worst that can happen?* I thought to myself. *I'll just take a swim.* Almost immediately I felt fear leave me. Racing forward, I heard the cheers of the other women and I knew in that moment that I had found my freedom. At first tentatively, and then with confidence, I let go of my grip on the cord, flung my arms wide open, and embraced the world as I flew through the air. The exhilaration of the ride was matched only by the joy in my heart as I released my hold on fear and embraced a new way of being. Although I had placed my trust in that which was tangible, namely, the zip line equipment, I realized that my real security could be found in my faith. It allowed me to leap into life, secure in the knowledge that I was being cared for by a power much greater than me.

I wasn't always this way. I had lost the ability to trust fully at a young age. As a result, I spent many years searching for something that was missing in my life. In some ways, I was like the woman described in a parable by Jesus who said, "What woman, having ten silver coins, if she loses one coin, does not light a lamp, sweep the house, and search carefully until she finds it? And when she has found it she calls her friends and neighbors together, saying, 'Rejoice with me for I have found the piece which I lost!' There is joy in the presence of the angels of God when one lost soul is found" *(Luke 15:8-10).*

There are many areas of my life where I have been lost —in relationships, in my career, and even in how I care for myself physically and emotionally. In the past, unaware of what was missing, I mindlessly made choices that took me in the wrong direction. I ended up wandering around in a fog until it slowly dawned on me that I was not where I wanted to be. Regardless of whether I strayed aimlessly or purposely—thinking I knew just what I needed—the result was always the same. I eventually found myself feeling lost, frightened, and very uncomfortable.

Interestingly, the most transformative lost experiences of my life have occurred when I felt stuck, trapped, and overwhelmed by my circumstances. Wanting to give up and hide from life's challenges, I often succumbed to fear and wondered in despair, *how did I get here?* Caught in a maze of my own misperceptions and doubts, I tried to force solutions to my problems. This often led to one dead end after another, as well as to a great deal of anxiety and frustration. Feeling out of control and unable to fix the situation or escape from it, I would eventually give up and cry out the most powerful prayer of all; "Help!" When I turned to God, a loving power much greater than myself, I was redirected on a journey of faith and trust.

I came into this world with a trusting nature; but even the most well-intentioned caregivers could not completely protect me from life's disappointments and harmful experiences. As a result, I noticed that I frequently danced between trust, and fear and doubt; perhaps you have as well. Although I may have valid reasons for being fearful at times, the truth is that being overly distrustful only caused me additional pain. I came to realize the importance of learning to trust again; not for the sake of others, but for myself. There are choices that I must make to gracefully flow from my fear and doubt to trust. Awareness is a critical first step. For much of my life, I denied that my fears existed and unknowingly let them control me. This is the path that led me to awaken from that denial and rediscover trust in myself, God, others.

Whether I have lost something tangible like keys, intangible like hope, or have gone off course myself, my reaction has been anxiety. I fearfully begin to retrace my steps both mentally and physically as I search for what is missing. The more difficult situations, which are not easily resolved, have caused me to wander for a time in a mental, emotional, or spiritual wilderness. With patience and persistence I eventually found hope, direction, and comfort from the two greatest commandments:

Love the Lord your God with all your heart, with all your soul, with all your mind, and with all your strength... the second is this, love your neighbor as yourself. There is no other commandment greater than these (Mark 12:30-31).

Loving others has never been difficult for me. In fact, sometimes I have focused too much on loving those around me, losing myself in caring for their needs. I used to believe that taking care of me was selfish. Yet the second commandment indicates that I will only be able to love others to the extent that I am able to love myself. Discovering my own worth and learning to love and accept myself has been a long journey, and it is one that I will be on for the rest of my life. However, I now recognize that caring for myself *is* God's will. With this knowledge, I can release thoughts of selfishness and nurture my uniqueness.

This is my story about being lost, and what I have found. My journey took me from one end of the reliance spectrum to the other. Initially I was overly dependent and expected others to be the source of my security. After experiencing some major life disappointments, I moved to the other end of the spectrum where I became overly independent, effectively distancing myself from others in order to feel safe and secure. Eventually feeling dissatisfied and uncomfortable, I began to question both extremes.

What would it be like to enter relationships without being so hungry for love that I lose myself in others?

And, alternatively, what would it be like to be less afraid of being close and to refrain from distancing myself emotionally from those I love?

This is a story, ultimately, of finding a balanced interdependence with others by first developing a relationship with myself and with God. I learned to achieve emotional security from conscious connections instead of relying on others, or entirely on myself.

How did I begin this journey? I began it with a decision to wake up. Like many people, I have at times led my life unconsciously, oblivious to what I was thinking or feeling. At other times I have doubted my own abilities and allowed fear and a lack of confidence to prevent me from engaging fully in life. My journey began when I chose to take responsibility for all of my growth; not just my mental or physical wellbeing, but also my emotional and spiritual development. Becoming self-aware has helped my heart, mind, and spirit awaken to a conscious and faith-based way of living. God-consciousness is the result of this heightened awareness and I find it to be enlightening, enlivening, and grounding all at the same time.

The benefits of faith-based living may be completely foreign to some. Others who see the value in it may allow the busyness of their lives to distract them from a regular and intentional connection with the Divine. Having been in each of these positions at various times in my life, I have found three simple yet powerful beliefs which help me achieve the consistent connection with God that I desire. When I regularly focus my attention on these beliefs, they grow stronger, much like an exercised muscle. As I use these three beliefs to center my personal faith, an inner strength grows deeper and deeper in me, similar to a sturdy tap root anchoring a tree.

You will find these centering beliefs woven throughout my story. As you read, I encourage you to notice them and to consider what effect they might have on your own faith story.

Three Centering Beliefs for Faith-based Living

I. God is personal and present. With this perspective I believe that God is available to everyone and wants to be in relationship with each of us. When I adopt this belief I focus on building a relationship through regular interactions with God to nurture and grow a personal awareness of the divine light within me. As I develop this relationship I learn to appreciate and accept the unique individual that I was created to be. Accepting my own talents and imperfections, in turn, allows me to see and acknowledge others for who they are, instead of how I may want them to be. As my awareness of a personal spiritual connection increases, it moves me to the second belief.

II. God guides and provides. Learning to lead a faith-based life means that I mindfully choose who I will follow. As I deepen my relationship with God I am better able to see how He takes care of me and offers guidance through my own inner wisdom. With this perspective there are no coincidences. Instead I see synchronistic occurrences as divine appointments and pause to consider what God is providing through the incident. This belief is grounded in prevenient grace; God's provision which precedes my knowing. I choose to believe that God is working for good even when I can't see or understand it. As I live from this perspective I partner with

God and trust that He is leading. This allows me to willingly let go of my need for control. Experiencing and deepening my understanding of the two beliefs provides a foundation for the third.

III: God heals our hearts swiftly and silently. With this perspective I acknowledge that wounded and broken hearts are part of the human experience. We all have them whether we admit it or not. The journey towards wholeness of heart, mind, body, and spirit includes the healing of those wounds. By practicing the first two principles regularly my heart has become more open and ready to be restored. Heart healings can occur in big or small transformative moments. Whether I feel them as powerful shifts or gentle washings of the heart, these rejuvenating experiences leave me feeling that everything is the same, yet everything is different; because I am different on the inside. Since I am a work in progress, these healing moments will continue throughout my life. Trusting that God is continually mending my heart allows me to remove my self-protective walls and engage in life more fully. I am better able to help and serve others when I am grounded in this source of ongoing renewal and replenishment.

These simple, yet profound, beliefs are the building blocks which have developed and maintained my faith and have cultivated a strength within me to face and overcome adversity.

God is personal and present.
God guides and provides.
God heals our hearts swiftly and silently.

With regular practice these beliefs orient and center me in a relationship with the Divine. Such a connection allows me to receive the many blessings this relationship has to offer and restores me to wholeness. From this full and overflowing place I am revitalized and ready to serve others with my own unique talents and gifts.

An Invitation for Self-Discovery

Wherever you are in your faith journey, I invite you to consider how these beliefs may impact you. How might they guide you to a greater understanding that you are a unique treasure, loved unconditionally by a God that you can trust? What would it feel like to find your heart's security in your relationship with the Divine instead of seeking this security entirely from others?

You have the opportunity to explore these inquiries and many others with this book. At the end of each chapter, you will find reflection questions that are designed to increase your awareness and growth. You may wish to answer the questions as you read or go back to them at a later time. Whichever way you choose to do it, I hope you will reflect and capture any new thoughts and feelings that my story may generate within you; perhaps by journaling or in conversation with a trusted spiritual friend, mentor, or advisor.

In my work as a professional coach, I frequently remind my clients that whatever we focus on grows. I would like to encourage you with the same concept. As you read, pay attention to your own energy and follow it. Notice which questions resonate with you and explore them as deeply as you like to further develop your own understanding. Remember to trust the process and allow it to unfold in whatever way is most meaningful to you.

I hope that *Lost and Found* will help you discover insights into your own faith story. Whether you wade into the waters of self-discovery slowly or jump in whole-heartedly, the choice is yours. This is *your* journey.

PART 1
Seeking

CHAPTER *1*

The Matchmaker

"Matchmaker, matchmaker, make me a match, find me
a find, catch me a catch..." – **Fiddler on the Roof**

W*hy am I here?* I asked myself for the umpteenth time
as I dialed back the windshield wiper speed yet again.
The blades made a rhythmic noise as they cleared the rapidly falling snow from my view and I carefully maneuvered
my car through the piles of wet slush that had accumulated
between the lanes of traffic. At least I wasn't the only crazy
(or adventuresome, depending upon how you looked at it)
person on the road. The weather report hadn't called for much
accumulation, so I had set out to keep my appointment with

a professional matchmaker in the Washington, DC area to see what good fortune it might bring.

It occurred to me several times that I should turn around and go home. The roads were getting pretty slick and I found myself questioning my sense of good judgment for traveling in such awful weather. As I ventured through the first half of the trip, an inner debate was going on inside my head. A voice of reason said, *This isn't smart or safe. Turn around and go back.* This was countered by another voice that urged me to stay on track and persevere. After all, I had attended college in New Hampshire and considered myself an adopted daughter of New England. I didn't have an aversion to snow; in fact, it delighted me. I wasn't afraid of a little accumulation on the road. This debate continued until I passed the halfway point, at which time my mind settled on the conclusion that I might as well press on to my destination, get it done, and then return home safely afterwards.

I was in it now.

Why was I here anyway? After seven years of being single, following a long and drawn out divorce, I was tired of being alone. There were times when it was fine, even good, to be on my own. I had grown in so many ways since ending my troubled marriage; this growth centered on rebuilding a life for me and my two sons. I had rediscovered myself, and I finally liked my life. But I still felt that something was missing.

I had tried online dating for a couple of years after my divorce and actually had a lot of great dates. I also experienced my share of bombs. I learned the process of reading through the profiles of potential candidates with the subsequent exchange of emails to get to know each other. Then the next step of talking on the phone would occur. If that went well, we would set a date to meet over coffee. This approach to dating was designed to go rather methodically, to ensure a sense of safety with the option of backing out at any point. As I drove, I reminisced about some of my more memorable encounters.

One of my favorite dates was with a man named George. After exchanging emails for some time, we decided to meet in person by the statue of Abraham Lincoln at the corner square in Gettysburg. Unbeknownst to either of us, the day we chose to meet was the anniversary of the night that Lincoln had stayed at the inn on this historic site. To mark the occasion, costumed re-enactors were parading all over town.

I arrived at the designated time, stood by the statue, and proceeded to look for a man who might have a curious expression on his face. Neither of us had a good idea of what the other one looked like, so there was an air of adventure about driving to this famous town to meet a man with whom I had only exchanged emails. Not long after I arrived, two women who were wearing long dresses and bonnets approached me and asked if I was Carol. When I said, "Yes" they giggled and informed me that a man named George had arrived 10 minutes earlier and had told them that we were meeting for a first date. They were delighted to be included in our story, and found it charming and exciting to help us find each other. There was something surreal about these women in costumes from the 1800's helping me to connect with a man I had met through the internet, and I laughed with them at the incongruity, and went to meet George for a lovely dinner.

My mind skipped ahead to another favorite date, this time with a man named Alan who lived on the other side of Maryland. Our designated meeting place was the Inner Harbor in Baltimore, where we sat at an outdoor table on a beautiful spring day and got to know each other. Hauntingly beautiful Peruvian pipe music filled the air, which lent a magical quality to the day. Alan was a charming man who had led quite an adventuresome life. He told me that he had spent the past 12 years living on a sailboat. I am a landlubber at heart, so his desire to sail around the world was both fascinating and foreign to me. After an entertaining afternoon together, we went our separate ways. Although I never saw him again, I didn't consider it a wasted day, because I enjoy meeting new people and getting to know them.

Typically, the disappointing dating experiences, which I like to refer to as bombs, were with men who either misrepresented themselves or who were still processing past relationships. I will never forget the time I was expecting someone with a full head of hair only to be told by the balding man before me that he had used a 10-year-old photo for his online profile. Frankly, I was not put off by his lack of hair but rather by his need to portray himself as something he was not.

Honesty is important to me, so this physical misrepresentation was concerning.

Other experiences I would categorize as bombs were dates with men who would spend an inordinate amount of time bashing previous partners or mourning the loss of their last relationship. I have always considered myself to be an attentive and compassionate listener, and I am accustomed to people processing their emotions out loud with me. However, nothing is quite so deflating to the hopefulness of a new relationship as being drawn into the toxic energy of someone's break-up. In those instances, I would be sympathetic and understanding for a reasonable amount of time. If my date couldn't change the subject to a more interesting and positive topic, I would conclude that he was not ready for a new relationship and draw our encounter to a close as gracefully as possible.

After online dating for some time, I grew weary of the effort it involved. Since I never settled down with one man for more than a few months, I decided to take a break from the process when I enrolled in coaching school. My plan was to re-enter the dating world after I completed my yearlong training and my youngest child went off to college.

When this time came, however, I found myself extremely busy with the task of building a new business. Work was certainly not as exciting as dating, but it was more predictable and secure. I dated an old friend off and on whenever I grew lonely for male company and this felt comfortable and safe.

Neither of us was willing to commit to anything further, however. I wasn't sure if I was just lazy about dating, or if I was letting the fear of being hurt prevent me from venturing back into the relationship arena.

For the most part, I was settled and content in my life, finally feeling comfortable in my own skin. But here I was, driving through a snowstorm on a December day in search of love. Why? Frankly, it started one Friday evening when I didn't have any specific plans. Feeling bored and a little lonely, I pulled out my laptop and decided to check out the online dating scene again. I visited a few websites and signed up for a Christian dating service, thinking it might provide some quality men with values similar to my own. I felt some ambivalence as I explored the site, however, and even considered the possibility that I might end up attracting overzealous men but continued anyway. Off to the side of the screen, I noticed a link for mature singles. I wondered what they meant by mature. Responsible? Old? Is there an age requirement for being considered mature? As a 50-year-old woman, I ventured a guess that I was in the appropriate age range and tentatively clicked on the link.

Immediately, I was presented with a list of basic questions. When I finished answering them, a brief statement popped up. It thanked me for completing the questionnaire and stated that someone would be calling shortly. Yikes! I didn't want to talk to anyone. I liked the control and anonymity of sitting comfortably in my recliner at home, knowing I could surf the web for love without actually talking to someone. I thought, *They had better not call me now; it's 11:00PM!* I snapped my laptop shut and went to bed, hoping that the phone wouldn't ring.

But the next day, I received a call from a dating service. The friendly woman on the other end of the line said that she was following up on my online inquiry. Since I was working from a home office and was in the middle of a project, I let my fear prevail and told her that it was not a convenient time to talk. I justified that I couldn't let my late-night longings for love interrupt my work day. I asked her to try me another time, secretly hoping that this would discourage her. Hanging up, I wondered if I would even answer the phone if she called back.

Later that night, she tried again. I decided to ignore my fear this time, and picked up the phone. Despite my initial reservations, it was a surprisingly affirming conversation. She took the time to ask me insightful questions about myself and my lifestyle, and seemed to really care about getting to know me. I found myself enjoying the interview and being honest with her about my dating history and what had prompted me to fill out the questionnaire.

When the interview was over, she explained that, as a dating service, her organization functioned differently than other online sites. It was standard policy to invite people to come into their office for an interview, to verify that candidates were representing themselves honestly. They did this to avoid the pitfalls of misrepresentation that can happen with online dating. 'Buyer beware' was the mantra of many websites, but this company's philosophy was to try to remove as much of the risk as possible. I was impressed (and a bit intimidated) when she told me that they conducted employment, credit, and legal checks. They even went so far as to verify that a candidate owned a car. This last requirement surprised me, and when I questioned it she said, "Well, would you want to date someone who didn't have it together enough to own their own car?" I thought it was an interesting way to measure a person's level of responsibility.

I didn't want to like this dating service, but the more I listened, the more I was drawn to the caring warmth conveyed by the voice on the other end of the line. It seemed that this woman was sincerely concerned about my welfare. She reassured me that her company checked all of their clientele in the same manner that she was screening me, so I could be confident in the quality of the men she would recommend. I had to admit that it was nice to have professionals looking out for my best interests. She then explained that the next step was for me to come in for an interview and proceeded to ask if I would like to schedule a time. I said, "Sure, why not?" What could be the harm in taking the next step? I could always stop the adventure at any time.

Several days later, I found myself sitting in the waiting room at the dating service, filling out pink forms on a clipboard. They asked about my education, employment history, finances, and health. You name it, they wanted to know it. I patiently completed each section and handed in my paperwork. After a short time, I was invited into a small, sterile office and took a seat across from a woman who introduced herself as Hannah. Again, I was prepared to stop this process at any moment and maintained an attitude of detached curiosity about the whole thing. We talked at length as she reviewed my forms and questioned me in a conversational manner. I was ready to dislike Hannah but I couldn't. She was warm, friendly, and approachable. I found myself opening up and honestly telling her about my love life since the end of my marriage. I even acknowledged that the anniversary of my divorce had recently passed and that I may be experiencing a new kind of seven-year itch. Enough with being alone, I was ready for a relationship now.

She then asked me a difficult question. "Do you have time to date?" *Do I have time?* I thought. *Why else would I be here?* But as I opened my mouth to speak, my frank answer surprised even me. "Based on how I live right now, probably not," I said. "I started a second career when my youngest son went off to college. It's something I am passionate about, and I spend as much time on it as possible. I sound like a workaholic, I know. Based on how I live right now, no, I don't make time to date." She asked if I was willing to make the time and I answered truthfully, "I don't know."

As Hannah looked back down at her papers and took notes, I knew the interview was all but over. She didn't think

I was a good candidate. I wasn't ready to give up, though, so I asked about their fees. I was hit squarely with the significant expense of hiring a dating service. For $4,000, I would receive 12 introductions over the course of two years. I was encouraged to have more than one date with each man and to move at my own pace, reporting back to the service with my impressions and feedback after each one.

Suddenly uncomfortable, I asked myself how I ended up in this office during the hectic weeks between Thanksgiving and Christmas, actually considering spending what I thought was an exorbitant fee to find a man. Why was this necessary? I left the interview with mixed emotions. Self-critical thoughts like *How desperate am I?* battled with *Wouldn't it be nice to have someone check my dates out for me and qualify them as men of integrity?* I had been deeply hurt by dishonest men too many times, and my lack of trust had caused me problems more often than I cared to admit. For the next few days, I contemplated joining this dating service, but then dismissed it based solely on the cost.

But I couldn't let go of the idea completely, and soon a thought popped into my head that maybe I should see if there were other companies that offered similar services, possibly at a more reasonable price. I started surfing the web again and found another site that looked promising. I decided to give them a call.

Similar to my first experience, I was subjected to another long but friendly phone interview. This was followed by an invitation to make an appointment to come into their office. I was honest with the woman on the phone and told her that I had already interviewed with one of their competitors and was shopping around for a better price. She replied that she was not allowed to discuss fees over the phone. I was adamant about knowing whether their fees were lower than the other service, which I named. "Yes, if you come in, we'll be sure to beat that price," she assured me. I trusted her and made the appointment for the following Saturday morning.

So here I was, in the middle of a snowstorm in early December, driving 50 miles to keep my appointment with a matchmaker. *How desperate am I?* I thought again. Obviously, desperate enough to venture out in heavy, wet snow when others were staying home, sipping hot cocoa. This was one of those times when I wondered whether I was displaying incredible stubbornness, or the more positive quality of perseverance. Whichever it was, I knew I wasn't going to give up. I couldn't turn around and go home, just to reschedule my appointment for another day. My time was much too precious.

So I carefully continued on to my destination. When I left the highway and started down the city streets, I hit stop-and-go traffic as buses and taxis navigated the slushy pavement. Pedestrians sloshed through piles of wet snow that were already turning gray from the passing cars that melted it with their exhaust. As I sat in a long line of traffic, waiting to snake through an intersection, my cell phone rang. It was a woman from the dating service, informing me that my contact was running late due to the weather. "Okay, I'm not worried about it," I said. "We'll both get there as soon as we can." As I made my way slowly through the city, I asked myself again, *Why am I here?* This time, I knew the answer. *I'm here because I'm not turning around now. I'm in this to the end. I am committed.*

Eventually, I came upon the office building where I was supposed to meet my contact. There was a hotel with an underground garage next door. I carefully turned in and drove down the short ramp to park, releasing a sigh of relief to be out of the weather. As I rolled down my window to take a ticket from the dispenser, I noticed that a car alarm was going off somewhere nearby. I tried to ignore it as I found a parking spot and looked for the nearest elevator. The shrill sound of the alarm was amplified and annoying as it echoed off the concrete walls. I wanted to exit the garage as quickly as possible to get to my meeting. On the way out, I stopped to ask the ticket cashier about the alarm that was going on and on. His accent was difficult to understand, but I could ascertain that he didn't know why the alarm was sounding or how to make it stop. I walked up the exit ramp, opening my umbrella as I ventured out into the falling flakes of snow. As I carefully stepped through the slippery mush, I felt grateful to be getting away from the incessantly screaming alarm.

I cut through the hotel lobby and out the other side, toward the building where my appointment was scheduled. I managed to work my way toward my destination, ducking under overhangs whenever possible to avoid stepping in piles of slushy, wet snow. As I entered the office building, I was struck by the fact that an alarm was going off there, too. *How strange. What are the odds of that?* I wondered. I also thought it odd that the building was so empty for a Saturday afternoon. I didn't see a single soul in the lobby or the hallways. I approached the elevator and pushed the button to go upstairs. However, the elevator didn't respond. Slowly, as if waking from a dream, it dawned on me that it wasn't a car alarm that was going off, but a building alarm. The parking garage was also connected to the building where I was supposed to meet the matchmaker, and both locations were loudly declaring that something was wrong. It occurred to me that I may not be safe standing in the lobby all by myself, so I exited the building and called my contact at the dating service. I left a message explaining the "alarming" situation in which I found myself, and said that I hoped he was not trapped somewhere in the upper floors of the office building. I informed him that I was headed next door to the hotel lobby and would wait for him there. I retraced my steps and entered the welcoming warmth of the bustling hotel, which sat above one of Maryland's busiest metro stops.

After a frustrating attempt to talk with the management about the alarm, I gave up and went in search of a hot cup of tea. I shook out my umbrella, sloughed off my dripping coat, and sank into a comfortable, deep chair. Within minutes, my cell phone rang again. It was Lyle, the matchmaker, who apologized profusely for keeping me waiting. He told me he was on the metro train, which would be pulling into the station downstairs shortly. I put him at ease and told him where I could be found when he arrived.

Lyle walked into the lobby shortly after our phone conversation. We exchanged a soggy handshake and apologized to each other for our mutual lateness. He was out of breath from literally running up the long escalator from the metro stop below. After I explained the situation with the alarms in the office building, he suggested that we hold our interview in the hotel and offered to buy me lunch. I agreed with a sigh of relief. It would feel good to sit and rest in the comfort of a cozy restaurant on such a blustery winter day.

As we settled into a booth, Lyle immediately started talking business. He began explaining the dating service to me, but I interrupted him, suggesting that we take a few minutes to just settle in. We had both become stressed over our trips to this meeting, and I knew I needed time to just be while I fixed my tea and prepared for the interview. My guess was that he felt the same way.

A handsome man in his early forties, Lyle mopped his brow as he tried to catch his breath. He explained that he was from Los Angeles but travels to the DC area once a week to conduct interviews because the head of the regional office here had recently left the company. He had borrowed a friend's car to drive to our appointment. Unfortunately, he had gotten stuck in the same kind of slow-moving traffic that I had encountered, and began to worry about being late. He finally decided it would be quicker to take mass transit, so he parked the car and descended underground. A train was exiting the station as he approached the platform, and he knew he would have to wait another seven minutes for the next one. When it finally came, he realized he was on the wrong side of the platform and had to run around to the other side, and then wait again for a train to be going in the opposite direction. He was clearly having one of those days when everything was going wrong. He was wet, tired, and frustrated when he ascended the escalator for our meeting, running two steps at a time while clutching his briefcase.

As I listened to him describe the ordeal he had been through, I actually began to feel guilty that I hadn't canceled my appointment. I felt as though my perseverance had put us both at risk and left us out of sorts. However, the hot tea was beginning to settle my nerves, and I tried to detach myself from my own harried morning as I listened with empathy to his story. It's strange, but there truly is comfort in knowing others are struggling, too.

After decompressing awhile, we shifted gears and began talking about the dating service. Perhaps our defenses were down after bonding over our stressful commutes, because he seemed to skip the formalities of interviewing. He asked me about myself and I openly shared that I had met with one of their competitors. I explained that I was interested in the concept of a dating service, but not excited about the price tag that came with it. He quickly told me that his company's fees were going to be higher than their competitor's. "What? How can that be?" I asked. "I *specifically* asked on the phone if it would be less expensive. I made it very clear that I didn't want to waste my time or yours discussing a service that I couldn't afford." I was upset, to say the least. I controlled my anger and conveyed it to Lyle in short sentences, pointing out that I felt misled. I think he actually smiled, and may have even been pleased to hear that his company's representative had gotten me to make an appointment, even though I had pushed her to reveal their prices on the phone.

Getting right to the point, he openly told me that their fees started at $5,000 and went as high as $25,000. One client even paid $50,000! Since I had experienced sticker-shock at the $4,000 mark, it is not hard to imagine how I paled at the thought of paying such an exorbitant amount of money to find a relationship. It was clear that I had come all this way for nothing, and I started to feel a sense of foolishness inside as I mentally berated myself. Unfortunately, we had already ordered lunch by this point in the conversation, and I felt obliged to stay and finish the meal.

Being an astute businessman, Lyle quickly realized that I was not a serious prospect for his company's services. Although he didn't apologize for his representative misleading me to the meeting, we were able to shift to a less threatening conversation about his business in general. This was no longer an interview but a luncheon exploration of the dating industry.

I have to admit that I was a bit fascinated as he shared his perspective. At one point in the discussion, I asked if many of the men in their database were from my hometown. He explained that they had clients from all over the United States. He went on to say that some of their clients own homes on both sides of the country, and don't think twice about going wherever a relationship may be available. He all but told me that I was thinking too small, limiting myself to only dating men near my hometown. I was slightly shocked at this thought, and immediately felt out of my league. *What am I doing here?* I asked myself again.

He eventually asked me the same question that I had encountered on my last interview. "How much time would you be willing to spend on dating?" When I honestly said, "I don't know. I hardly spend any time on it right now," I saw the familiar dismissive look in his eyes. Again, I was being perceived as not ready to be committed to serious dating.

I felt even more unsettled when Lyle went on to say that women my age were hard to match. He looked me over, and in a rather detached voice told me that I obviously took good care of myself and looked younger than my real age. "You're well groomed, attractive, and pay attention to your appearance. You don't look 50," he said. I felt both flattered and irritated by his blatant judgment of me.

Clearly Lyle had decided that I was not going to sign up for the service when he went on to say that my file could easily slip through the cracks. He informed me that men typically look for younger women. Recognizing that what he said was true, I nodded my head in agreement and asked, "Why is that?" With a quick shrug of his shoulders he said, "Because they can." His arrogance was getting to me and I decided it was time to end our meeting. I had tried to listen courteously, ask questions, and be engaged in the conversation, but I had had enough of his disrespectful comments. It was time to leave.

Lyle paid the check and as we walked out of the restaurant he shifted back into sales mode. He said that he highly recommended that I consider their $20,000 plan because it came with a lifetime guarantee. I would have an unlimited number of matches, as many as I needed until I found the right man. I balked again at the price, and he told me the story of a school teacher who, despite a limited income, was able to save enough money to choose this option. I reiterated to him that I wasn't willing to spend that much money. As we walked through the hotel lobby, he made his last sales pitch and dropped the price in half. "Carol, I like you and I want to help make this happen for you. So for just $10,000, you can have our $20,000 program." I shook his hand, said, "No thanks," and walked away.

As I drove home, I mentally kicked myself for wasting my time on this wild-goose chase. I could have been doing so many more productive things with my day, especially with Christmas less than a month away. *What was I thinking coming down here?* I continued to berate myself for several miles and then started to see some humor in the situation. God had clearly been trying to tell me *not* to go on this tangent. Between the snowstorm, the traffic, and the screaming alarms, you'd think that I would have gotten the message that this was not a good idea. Unfortunately, I had ignored all of the signs, insisting on doing what I wanted to do.

As a coach, I encourage my clients to learn from their experiences. So I asked myself, *what lesson can I take away from this?* With this new perspective, I was soon chuckling and shaking my head at my own stubborn insistence on trying to make this happen on my time schedule.

As doubts crept into my mind, and I actually started to reconsider Lyle's final offer, I had a moment of sudden clarity. I realized that I have the greatest matchmaker that exists. I believe that God is working to develop abundant love and blessings in my life, and that I simply have to trust His timing and His guidance. The adventure I had just encountered was clearly *not* a God-led time; it was a Carol-led time. Trying to make it happen, I had gone traipsing off in a direction of my choosing. I was looking for what I needed outside of my-

> I realized that I have the greatest matchmaker that exists.

self, when all that I really needed was inside of me. Feeling reconnected to my trust in God's plan for my life, I went home with a smile on my face. I was confident that He would lead me to my next relationship if I remained open and willing to trust. The truth is that for me, this was much easier said than done.

"So, how'd it go?" asked my friend Laura, as we sat in a coffee shop the following week.

"Not good," I replied. "What a waste of time. I can't believe I went all the way down there, through that crazy storm, just to find out it would cost me twenty grand to find a man. Who needs that? I'm just not that desperate yet."

"Wow, that does sound steep," she said, "But you know, I'd pay that amount for my husband. He's totally worth it."

Not for the first time, I looked at Laura with eyes of wonder. "Really? Do you mean that? You'd pay that much money to have a series of dates to find the man of your dreams?"

"Absolutely," was her reply. I shook my head in amazement at this woman who so openly treasured her husband. I felt a surge of envy and longed for a relationship of my own that had such compatibility, respect, partnership, and love. She was one of the lucky ones.

I know many women who are scarred by broken relationships and divorce; they wear a protective shield of cynicism and have a general distrust of men. It was refreshing to hear Laura boldly declare how much she valued the man in her life. In my gut, I knew how badly I wanted that type of relationship for myself. I just had to overcome the fears that had been instilled in me through negative life experiences. As I drove away from the coffee shop that day, I once again reminded myself that I have the greatest matchmaker in the world. I chose to believe that God would bring the next relationship into my life. My responsibility was to remain patiently open to possibilities and see what He provided. Even with this new and receptive perspective, I almost missed it.

CHAPTER ONE
REFLECTION QUESTIONS
Discovering Guidance

1. What are your beliefs about guidance coming from a Higher Being ?

2. In what ways have you experienced such guidance in your life?

3. What stumbling blocks have you encountered when you have tried to 'make something happen'?

4. What do you know about forcing solutions?

CHAPTER 2

Matchmaker for Life

S omething shifted for me when I surrendered to God that snowy day in December. It wasn't just my love life that I gave over to Him. I made a conscious decision to *let go and let God* and to trust that He had a plan for me even when I couldn't see all of it. I accepted that my role in this partnership with the Divine was to follow the nudges given to me each day by listening to the whisperings of my heart and the guidance of my spirit. It meant surrendering my will to God's will; requiring me to lead with my heart and not my head. Observing my intuition first and considering my mind second in order to support these heartfelt instincts isn't always easy, but the more I do it, the more I see how well it works in my life.

The shift first began to happen in my work, when a 10-year-old dream of holding a retreat for women started to fall into place. It began with the daydream of opening a coffee shop somewhere in town. As different buildings became available for occupancy, I would invite a friend to go with me to see them. Parked outside (sometimes in the pouring rain), we would gaze at the building and imagine how to turn it into an inviting space where people could gather and take yoga classes, meditate, or just sit to read or write. I would offer classes for young mothers to have a break from their children, while providing reading circles for the little ones. I envisioned a place that would nurture women; encouraging them to relax and reconnect with themselves.

Eventually, I realized this dream wasn't about coffee at all. It was about creating a space for women to feel nurtured and to grow. It was about making powerful connections that would help women awaken and become aware of whom they were so that they wouldn't lose themselves in the demands of family or work; something I myself had done years ago. I had shared this dream for many years with family and friends. But since becoming a coach, I found myself talking about it with complete strangers as well. I dreamed aloud of hosting an event that would cultivate women's outer beauty (through makeup, skin care, jewelry, etc.) with their inner beauty (through a variety of personal development topics). My goal was to help women see that, while outer care can be fun, it is our inner qualities that really make us beautiful. It is who we are that creates beauty, not what we look like. As I talked about my ideas, several women said to me, "When you make that happen, I want to attend." There were also a few who said, "When you do that, I want to help make it happen."

One woman, in particular, was pivotal to my dream becoming a reality. Jeanette was a success coach with whom I enjoyed a professional friendship. Over breakfast one day at a diner, we chatted amiably about our growing coaching businesses. I shared with her my vision of providing a day retreat for women. I envisioned offering personal and professional development workshops as well as opportunities for participants to learn about and even try alternative practices for their physical well-being, such as acupuncture, massage, and reflexology. Not only would our guests benefit from this experience, but so would the coaches and practitioners who demonstrated their services. I dreamed of a win-win situation for everyone involved.

As I spoke passionately about what I wanted to do, Jeanette said, "Carol, you're a mover and a shaker and I want to do this with you. Let's do it!"

"Really? You mean that?" I asked, in surprise.

She looked me squarely in the eye and replied simply and clearly, "Really."

And so it began.

Throughout the fall, Jeanette and I met often and started developing our retreat plans. At the start of the New Year, I suggested that we invite those women who had expressed an interest in helping to make my dream a reality. So, on a cold January day, I built a fire in my fireplace, put the kettle on for tea, set out some refreshments, and hosted my first Wholistic Coaching Coalition meeting. The women who attended (Sandie, Kelye, Lisa, and Laura) were enthusiastic and eager to help Jeanette and me. Our group began to hold weekly meetings to create what would become a fabulous retreat experience for the whole woman; one that integrated awareness of body, heart, mind, and spirit.

It amazes me how God brings the right people into my life at just the right time. I am continuously impressed by the fact that each woman in the coalition brought a set of skills and traits that benefited the whole group. As we worked together to create the retreat in three short months, we grew to care for one another and for the women who we would be nurturing. Self-care became the theme of the retreat and we reminded one another to practice what we preached. Our coalition had become a community of support and grace as we encouraged one another to grow and evolve individually while we were also growing as a group.

At the conclusion of the inaugural Wholistic Woman Retreat, I stepped to the podium, deeply satisfied and excited to address the 45 women who had joined us on the first day of spring in the Catoctin Mountains of Maryland. On this day, my desire to create a retreat had come true. The dream I had inside of me for 10 years didn't blossom until I gave voice to it and started speaking about it with more and more people. It was a vision that attracted individuals who could enliven it. In creating this retreat, I had learned an important lesson. I had traveled the spectrum from being in a dysfunctional codependent marriage riddled with anxious attachment to being a strong, capable, independent woman. The lesson God had for me now was interdependency. By sharing responsibilities and joys with others, I realized that I was able to accomplish much more than I could ever do on my own.

I asked the audience that day, "Who is your team? Who can help you make your dream come true? What help do you need and who can supply that help?" Because some dreams are just too big to do alone.

Likewise, who makes up your team when life is hard and challenging? Who do you call on when you are overwhelmed and freaking out? At the retreat, I shared an experience that had occurred just five days earlier, when my sump pump had failed during heavy rain and snow melt. Six inches of water quickly flooded my finished basement.

I can handle many types of crises. Those that involve water, however, present a serious challenge for me. Due to several near-drowning experiences as a child, out-of-control water situations send me first into freeze mode, and then I utterly and completely fall apart. I become overwhelmed and unable to think clearly, which leads to great distress and a flood of tears. Despite my angst that day, I felt a sense of relief when help arrived almost immediately. My son Ben had called several of our neighbors, who quickly arrived at our house with towels and a wet vac. Although their efforts couldn't handle the volume of water that was seeping into my house, I was reassured by the fact that they were there for me with concern in their eyes and hands ready to help in any way possible. We carried the important items upstairs and started to troubleshoot the cause of the problem. I continued to sob, but not as heavily as before, and I started to see that God had sent these water-angels to help me through an overwhelming situation.

In my concluding remarks to the women at the retreat, I shared my stories about teamwork and the value of interdependency. I summarized that the lesson was that whether I am building a dream, dealing with a hassle, or facing a serious challenge, I don't have to do it alone. God intends for us to live in community so that we can receive the support that we need. Adopting this approach to my work, and ultimately to my life, took me through a transformational gateway to a much more satisfying world of connectivity, where buds of trust were able to grow. Believing that God is my matchmaker in all areas of my life, I see how He continually brings me the people I need every day. It is my responsibility to remain open to recognize, interpret, and accept what is being provided.

CHAPTER TWO
REFLECTION QUESTIONS

Discovering Your Team

1. In what area of your life do you tend to be overly independent and what impact does it have on your relationships?

2. Anxious attachment, or feeling overly needy of others, is not uncommon at times. What would be one small step you could take towards depending more on God in anxious relationships?

3. In what relationships do you experience interdependence with others?

4. Who is on your support team when you face life's challenges?

5. What would it be like to believe that God is your matchmaker; providing the people that you need at just the right times in your life?

6. What would it be like to trust that God is working for good in all things, even when you can't readily see it?

CHAPTER 3

Seeds of Faith

For many of us, seeds of faith are planted in childhood but don't sprout until certain experiences test us later in life and become catalysts for our growth.

My earliest memory of such a seed was in 1967. I was with my mother and my sister Sally at our little country church. Wearing a blue pinafore dress, anklets, and shiny black patent leather shoes, I have an envelope with my Sunday school offering in my white, child-sized purse. I watch my mother, imitating her actions and appearance; absorbing the lessons that she is teaching me. Whether she is aware of it or not, she is my role model for womanhood.

Today, I am excited because I have been memorizing the 23rd Psalm, and this is the day that I get to recite it. I call a quick goodbye to Mom over my shoulder and race downstairs to the Sunday school rooms to find my teacher, Mrs. Dixon.

I know God best through Sunday school. When I sit with my mother in Sunday services, the pastor's voice seems to drone on forever, and my mind drifts away. I can't relate to what he is saying, and I daydream about other things during worship time. It is in Sunday school, however, that I am able to interact with thoughts and images of God. We read about Him and color pictures of famous Biblical scenes.

My childlike image of God is of an old man with a white beard, sitting on a throne in heaven, somewhere high in the clouds above me. He is magnificent, distant, and a bit intimidating in His authority and grandeur. I feel small and vulnerable in comparison to this detached image.

Recently, Mrs. Dixon has been encouraging us to memorize Bible verses and recite them for her. We receive a gold star on a chart for each verse that we say correctly. Up to this point, I have been half-hearted in my attempts at memorization. However, there is something that I like about the 23rd Psalm. Somehow, it makes God more real and less distant for me.

In my eight-year-old voice, I softly recite, "The Lord is my Shepherd, I shall not want. He makes me lie down in green pastures; He leads me beside the still waters; He restores my soul..." I feel reassured and closer to God as I speak these ancient lines. "I will fear no evil; for You are with me. Your rod and Your staff, they comfort me." The promise of these words fills my heart and it expands as I savor the presence of God in these holy verses. With a childlike innocence, I finish, "Surely goodness and mercy shall follow me all the days of my life; and I will dwell in the house of the Lord forever. Amen."

My teacher congratulates me and I am rewarded with a sticker for my successful memorization. After class, I happily tell Mom and Sally about it and then skip to the car, carefree and secure in my little world; feeling connected to God.

Time has a way of changing us though, and three years later I am at a different point in my life. Now 11 years old, I am complaining that I have to go to church. I am grumbling in protest and questioning why my father and older brother get to stay home on Sunday mornings and I can't. My mother, who was raising six children between the ages of 2 and 14, is often frazzled and overwhelmed. She decides to give me a choice, just as God gives us a choice about being in relationship with Him.

In an assertive tone she says, "I'm going to church on Sunday mornings and anyone who wants to come with me is welcome to do so." I let out a whoop, taking this statement as permission to stay home on Sundays and sleep late. My father is vocally anti-church, believing that it is just an organization that wants to take his money and offers no real benefit. Dad and Mom have an understanding; church is something that she likes to do and he doesn't, so they each do their own thing on Sunday mornings. In my pre-adolescent years, I choose not to go, thinking I have just hit the jackpot and won something great. I've been let off the hook and released from the obligation of church.

This decision feels good for a while, but by age 13 I am seeking God again. Our family of eight often expanded to include others because my parents lived by the philosophy: "There is always room for one more." It was not unusual to have friends visit with us for a weekend or even an extended period of time, our house providing a safe place for them to stay while they sorted through challenges in their own lives.

Our large country home was a welcoming place, with half a dozen children, three dogs, an assortment of other pets, and a steady stream of visitors. My mother was a saint; feeding hoards of people on a regular basis. Our home was understandably chaotic, with running children, squeals of laughter, and the occasional physical and emotional bumps that come with so many people living together under one roof.

Being in the middle of such a large family, I often struggled to find my voice and to be heard. When I needed solitude, I would escape the noise and venture outdoors into the woods that surrounded our home. Taking long walks in those woods, I absorbed the quiet and breathed in the earthy scents as the leaves crunched under my feet. I would talk out loud to the canopy of trees above me.

My teenage fears, heartaches, and troubles would tumble out as I shared them with a Presence in the woods. I didn't know with whom I was speaking. I just felt compelled to express myself in this space where I felt small and insignificant, and yet, seen and heard. The Presence felt both high above me and close inside me at the same time. Feeling heard on a deep level, I would return from these walks renewed and peaceful. It was in nature that I first found my voice and began to make a personal connection with something much larger than myself.

I also found this God connection in music; specifically, in the 1970's rock opera, *Jesus Christ Superstar*. Mom took Sally and me to see it at a theater-in-the-round, and we fell in love with the songs. We bought the album and quickly memorized every word as we played it over and over on our record player. We were basement performers, dividing the parts between us and singing along at the top of our lungs.

At holiday gatherings, when my cousins would visit, we'd have a more substantial cast. We would practice our parts for hours, and then put on a show after dinner for all of the adults. My cousin Kathleen, Sally, and I would croon along to Mary Magdalene singing, "I don't know how to love him..." and it was so true. Our innocent young hearts longed for an understanding of the love God showed us through Jesus; a concept we had not yet begun to grasp. We knew every word of that rock opera, and although it was a superficial understanding of Christ's life, at least it offered something during those years when I had drifted away from a faith community.

Fast forward a few more years and I am 16 years old, driving home from school in my bright orange Volkswagen station wagon with my best friend Amy seated beside me. It's

Friday, and Amy will be spending the weekend at my house. We have big plans to go to a field party that night with my older brother and his friends. As Amy turns the radio dial, scanning the airwaves for our favorite rock station, we talk excitedly about boys and who we'll see at the party. The dial lands on a Christian station, and the DJ is talking to his listeners about salvation. "Oh, Jesus!" Amy exclaims in a flippant voice. I laugh with her and say, "Quick turn the station," as if it is some plague upon the earth to listen to such preaching.

Honestly, I just didn't get the whole Jesus thing. I was attracted to his radical long hair and sandals, but was turned off by preachers who pushed their points of view on others in an imperative and superior way. In my rebellious teenage years, I was fully irreverent, and disdainful of religion and church doctrine. I embraced the 'God is love' and 'peace' spirituality of the 1970's, but rejected the authority of the church, which told me what to believe and how to live my life. Although I hadn't totally abandoned the concept of God, I was a long way off from His Presence as I pursued my own selfish desires of love, peace, and the hippie lifestyle. I was a consummate flower child, lost in a daydreaming world of self-centered pleasures. I thought I had it all together and didn't need God.

The spiritual seeking that I had done when I was 13 had been replaced with fast living amongst a sex, drugs, and rock-n-roll crowd. I was immersed in short-term answers to my aching need for love and acceptance. I sought connections through physical relationships and other heightened ethereal experiences that were brought on by alcohol and drugs, and distanced myself from all things spiritual.

These were the 'lost years' when my desire to be close to God grew very dim. Minimizing my need for Him, I filled the God-void inside of me with partying and romantic relationships, thinking I was having the time of my life. College brought more of the same behavior, and I only remembered God's presence when I hiked in the mountains of New Hampshire. My single connection to Him during my college years was the awestruck wonder that I experienced in nature, and I became an avid photographer trying to capture this with my camera. Whether it was the vastness of a magnificent mountaintop view or the intricacies of a flower or insect, I was aware that something or someone had created these things. God had become present for me in His Creation.

The year was 1983, and I was in love and planning my wedding. I was ready to commit my life and future to marriage with a special man named Matt. I found myself wanting and needing to reconnect with the small country church from my childhood, so I asked my mother if it would be possible to go back there for my wedding. She encouraged Matt and me to talk with the new pastor, so we made an appointment to meet with him for pre-marital counseling. We entered the office and sat in two chairs that were facing his desk. Behind him was a window which provided a view of a verdant garden. My nervousness eased when I saw the lush green trees, which served as a backdrop for this man of God. Over the course of several visits, Pastor Dave talked with us about marriage, and we made a decision to have him perform the ceremony.

Despite being very happy together, Matt and I had some spiritual issues to sort out. He was raised Catholic, had been through a divorce, and had a five-year-old son named Mickey. I was happy to embrace his family and create a place in my heart and life for his child. I was not very comfortable, however, with his religion. I was put off by the fact that the Catholic Church didn't accept me and would not recognize our marriage. Fortunately, Matt was perfectly agreeable to being married in the Presbyterian Church instead. Despite encouraging visits with Pastor Dave, I was not sure why I wanted to be married in a church. At the time, I felt that I was being a bit hypocritical, but I couldn't deny the inner nudge to take this important step in a traditional way, before God and other witnesses, as we started our married life together. Although God seemed very distant, I still felt that getting married in a church was important at this crossroad of my life. And so we did.

A few years later the birth of our son Patrick brought much laughter and joy to our lives. Once more, an unexpectedly compelling urge arose within me to return to the church; this time to get my child baptized. Despite feeling hypocritical again, I began talking with Matt about finding a place of worship in our area. He agreed and we began church shopping.

Out of respect for Matt's upbringing, we attended several services at the local Catholic Church. I still didn't feel welcome or accepted, and suggested that we visit other congregations. He graciously agreed and we attended service at a large United Methodist church in the center of town. It was a cathedral-style building, impressive in size and presence. The high ceilings, plush red carpet, and stained glass windows were beautifully grand and vastly different from the quaint country church that I had attended as a child. I entered the building with hushed reverence, slightly intimidated by its architectural magnificence. However, I received such a warm, sincere welcome from its members that I was immediately put at ease. We attended services several times over the next few months and came to know the new pastor, assistant pastor, and director of Christian Education, who were members of a recently formed leadership team. Matt and I both thought that it was exciting to be there at the start of a new era. We decided to join this welcoming community and Patrick was baptized soon after.

Friendships formed with other young families as we participated in social activities at the church. Matt and I started attending regularly to see our friends and connect with this growing faith community. Four years later, we were blessed with another son, Ben, and the decision to have him baptized there came easily. As my comfort level increased with this faith community, I joined the Family Life Planning Committee and was a member of the leadership team that developed and organized various fun events, including chili cook-offs, hoedown dances, Christmas craft fairs, and family retreats. Matt and I participated in an adult Sunday school class, and found the weekly discussions about parenting issues and faith formation enlightening and supportive in our role as parents.

Interestingly, many of us in the class were intimidated by the Bible. Whenever our study guide suggested that we reference Scripture, we would skip over that section, limiting our conversation to a more general view of the material, which felt non-threatening. We benefited from the weekly discussions, but didn't get as much out of our study as we could have if we had explored the Word of God.

Eventually, Matt and I acknowledged our avoidance of the Bible, and decided to take a big step and join a Disciple Bible Study class. This required a major commitment, as the class met once a week for 36 weeks, from September until June. The goal was to read the Bible from Genesis to Revelation. Busy with our blended family of three sons, we felt that we hardly had the time to devote to such an undertaking. Encouraged by our peers, however, we accepted the challenge, along with several other couples who were also raising young children.

Fortunately, not only were these weekly gatherings enriching for the parents, but they were entertaining for the children. The little ones played happily in the nursery and became good friends while we studied God's Word and discussed questions that arose from our readings during the week. The class was made up of 12 members and was led by our associate pastor, a young man fresh out of seminary who was full of enthusiasm and encouragement. Our group consisted of four couples with young children, balanced by three women and one man (all in their sixties or seventies) who had led long lives of faith and were well acquainted with the Bible. This was a special group of people who had a profound impact on me. Taking this class was a major turning point in my faith and understanding of God. It was the most rewarding Bible study I had ever done.

One of the main gifts that I received from the class was the elimination of my fear of the Bible. As I regularly studied this ancient book, I became more confident in my ability to open it and find what I needed within its pages. Not since I had memorized the 23rd Psalm as a child did I feel so connected to the wisdom of God. By studying the Bible from beginning to end, I began to understand the relationship between the Old and New Testaments. I saw the progression of God's interaction with humanity, and started to understand how Jesus fit into the picture.

For years I had said, "I get God, and I get the Holy Spirit, but I just don't get Jesus. He just seems like a story character to me." I understood God to be an omnipresent Being that was more immense than we could imagine, yet who appeared in the very minutest details of life. I understood the Holy Spirit to be those inner nudges, the guidance that I had in my life when I just knew which direction or action to take. I had chosen my homes, my friends, and even my spouse trusting my gut. I now called that wisdom the Holy Spirit. Although I still didn't get Jesus, as I continued to study the Bible, my understanding of Him began to grow.

I especially liked the story in which Jesus overturned the tables at the market in anger because it made Him seem so human to me. I also enjoyed reading about Mary and Martha because I could relate to these two sisters. Martha fussed over what her guests would eat and drink and was jealous of Mary, who sat by Jesus' feet listening to his teachings. I thought I was more like Martha, so it was reassuring to me when Jesus was kind to them both, even though it was clear that Mary was making the better choice. I needed this wisdom in my own life, and I began to consider my Bible study time as my Mary-time. I could relate to many of the characters in the Bible stories and felt reassured that if God could love and accept them, then perhaps He would do the same for me.

As we read both the Old and New Testaments, I saw the complexity of God and His relationship with humankind throughout history. I was surprised at the range of emotions found in this Book, which sometimes read like a soap opera. It contained a cast of characters that lied, cheated, murdered, raped, and betrayed one another, underscoring the less savory side of humanity. The seemingly wrathful God of the Old Testament was unfamiliar to me, and reading these sections was fascinating yet uncomfortable. As we transitioned to the New Testament, however, I understood how the love and compassion of Jesus, who was God in human form, was needed.

The older members of our class were fountains of wisdom, offering their perspectives and insights as the younger members wrestled with some of the content we read. I especially struggled with the many references to fearing God, and I expressed my confusion about these verses in class. One of the older women, Joyce, shared her perspective with me that the word *fear* in this context meant to be in awe of God. Her insights helped me think about fear in a new way as I turned the concept over in my mind. The following week, Joyce came to class with a sheet of notebook paper that was filled with Scripture references about fearing God. She had painstakingly researched and handwritten the many ways in which we are instructed to fear (or be in awe of) God. I didn't fully understand what she meant, but I was touched by the kind gesture. I deeply appreciated that she cared enough to devote her time and energy to help me better understand God and His Word.

Joyce gave me a gift that has lasted for many years. Not only did she shift my perspective about fearing God, but she also modeled how an elder in faith can provide valuable guidance to a younger one on a spiritual journey.

CHAPTER THREE
REFLECTION QUESTIONS
Discovering Your Spirituality

1. What would a timeline of your faith look like?

2. Describe your deepest spiritual connections. How, when, and where did they occur?

3. What individuals or communities support your spiritual growth, either currently or in the past?

CHAPTER *4*

A Crisis that Transforms

As so often happens in our faith walks, a major crisis in December of 1993 taught me lessons about God in ways that I couldn't possibly have imagined. My husband traveled to New Jersey one weekend to be with his father, who was scheduled to undergo heart surgery. This was one of the weekends when Mickey was with his mother and I had just Patrick and Ben with me. I hugged Matt goodbye, and like so many of us do when we bid farewell to our loved ones, I assumed that I would see him again in a few days.

After Matt left and the children were tucked in bed, a friend from church, Baerbel, came by to watch a movie with me. We were sitting and chatting when the phone rang. It was my father-in-law, who informed me that Matt was in the emergency room being prepped for surgery. In my shocked state, I began blurting out questions. "What happened? What are they doing? Why does he need surgery?" My flustered father-in-law said that he didn't have any more information than what he had just told me, but would call back with more details as soon as possible. My hand shook as I hung up the phone, and in complete disbelief I whispered, "Oh, dear God, help." I had just seen Matt less than seven hours ago. I simply could not comprehend the news that I had just received.

A short time later, I received a call from Matt's brother-in-law, Jonathan, who is a doctor. He slowly and calmly explained that my husband was undergoing exploratory surgery. He was bleeding internally and they didn't know why. I tried to process what I was being told, but my mind was dazed and confused. I felt completely befuddled. Jonathan gently asked, "When can you be here?"

"What? When can I be there? I don't know. Do I need to be there?" I replied, not fully grasping the gravity of the situation.

"Yes," he said firmly. "I'll keep you informed, but you need to make plans to get here." I hung up the phone and looked at Baerbel as the frightening reality began to sink in. She hugged me and we prayed together. I would say that God stepped in and took over at that point, but the reality is that He had already provided for me by ensuring that I wasn't alone that night. I began making phone calls. I spoke to Mom and Sally and they asked what they could do to help.

My mind was in freeze mode and all I could say was, "I need you to help me think. I just can't think right now. How am I going to get to New Jersey tonight?" The night was pitch black, and there was a veritable deluge falling outside. The rain pounded on the roof furiously as I considered what to do with my two children, who were sleeping peacefully upstairs. Since I was still physically shaking, I knew I was in no condition to drive.

A team soon evolved from the people that God placed in my life that night. Baerbel offered to stay overnight with Patrick and Ben. Sally called the airports to ask about flights, and then reported back to me that none were available. News of my predicament spread among family and friends, and within a few hours a clear plan was in place. Vinnie and Dave, who were the husbands of my two dear friends, Tricia and Pat, would drive me the 50 miles to Baltimore, where I would catch a train to New Jersey. Baerbel would sleep on the couch, and Tricia would arrive in the morning to care for the boys and explain to them why I wasn't there. Tricia was like a second mother to them, and I knew they would be reassured by her presence.

My brother, Paul, who lived in New Jersey, would pick me up at the train station and drive me to the hospital. There, I would meet up with Matt's sister, Mary Kay, who was also a doctor. With the plan in place, I quickly threw some belongings into a suitcase. My packing was interrupted by another call from Jonathan, who told me that Matt was out of surgery and stable for the time being. I momentarily breathed a sigh of relief, only to take another quick breath in as he asked, "When can you be here?" I explained my plans and then hurriedly said, "I thought you said he was stable." Jonathan's reply, "He is. *For now...*" left me feeling reassured and anxious at the same time.

I kissed my sleeping children goodbye and ran through the downpour to the waiting van. I thanked Vinnie and Dave for driving me to Baltimore in such terrible weather. I felt it was truly above and beyond the call of duty and expressed my heartfelt gratitude. I filled them in on as many details as possible, and then we all fell silent. The slapping of the windshield wipers was the only sound as they rapidly cleared the sheets of water descending on the van. We each silently contemplated the seriousness of the situation. In my mind, I pondered the unfathomable possibility of life without my husband.

When we arrived at the train station, I expected Vinnie and Dave to just drop me off at the door, but they insisted on parking and escorting me inside. It was 2:00 AM and there were only a few other people waiting for the train. The cavernous halls of Penn Station echoed around us as we sat on the hard benches and talked quietly. The attendant told us that not many people took this train and that its main purpose was to move the mail. It felt surreal to be sitting there in the middle of a rainy night, waiting to catch a mail train to

New Jersey, something I couldn't have foreseen or anticipated earlier that day.

Once I boarded the train, I was on my own for four hours. This was the first time I was alone since getting the call from my father-in-law. Looking back, I can see that God had provided every person who helped me that night. Traveling in the dark to New Jersey, I sat and prayed for Matt, for my sons, and for myself. I prayed for the doctors and nurses who were attending to my husband, and for my in-laws and those who were supporting them.

Exhausted, I soon dozed off, lulled by the gentle rhythm of the train. I awoke suddenly as the conductor passed by shouting, "Newark Station!" Startled and confused, I leapt to my feet thinking, *That's my stop!* I began to tremble, realizing that I had almost slept through it, and said a quick prayer of thanks that I had heard the conductor's call. I reached for my bag, exited the train, and went in search of my brother. It was 7:00 AM and Paul was at the station, waiting for me in his car. As we started the hour-long drive to the Jersey shore, I told him all that I knew about Matt's condition. When we arrived at the hospital, I was relieved when Paul insisted on coming inside with me. I didn't know what I would be facing, and it was reassuring to have my brother there to support me.

We made our way to the ICU waiting room, where we were met by my sister-in-law, Mary Kay. She greeted me with a hug and quickly updated us on Matt's condition. It was

9:00 AM and he was in the ICU and still stable. However, his condition was tenuous, at best. Unable to identify the source of his internal bleeding, the doctors had performed exploratory surgery and found a ruptured aneurysm in Matt's splenetic artery. They had lost him several times on the table when his blood pressure bottomed out. Mary Kay explained that the first 24 hours after such major surgery was a crucial time.

As we slowly walked towards the recovery room, she asked me if I'd ever been in a hospital before. "Just for childbirth," I replied. She calmly explained that people swell quite a bit after major surgery and that I should expect Matt to be unrecognizable in this condition. I tried to brace myself and entered his room. Even with Mary Kay's warning, I was unprepared for the impact of the next few moments.

I could hardly see Matt under all of the equipment and tubes. I immediately went to his bedside and whispered to him that I was there. Even though he was unconscious and breathing through a tube, I knew that he felt my presence. I reached for his hand but could only grab his fingertips, due to all of the machines that were keeping him alive.

My head grew faint with the effects of seeing him so physically compromised, and I entered a second stage of shock. I backed away, sat down, and put my head between my knees. Out of the corner of my eye, I saw Paul quickly leave the room as dizziness overcame him as well. I pulled off my heavy sweater and felt revived by the cool air. I took some time to adjust as the reality of the situation settled upon me. I had been so focused on getting to Matt's bedside that I hadn't really anticipated what I might find when I got there. It was worse than I had imagined. This robust, healthy man, whom I had just hugged the day before, was now hanging onto life by a thread. I had been in constant prayer since receiving the call the previous night. I sat by his bedside and spoke quietly to him, trusting that he could hear me.

Matt spent three days in the ICU. During that time, I had the opportunity to talk with the surgeon who had performed the operation. He explained that during such emergency surgery, when physicians don't know what they're looking for, they make a zipper incision from chest to navel. He went on to say that aneurysms are typically found in the brain or in the main aortic blood vessel. Matt's aneurysm, however, was not in one of these usual places. So in this dire situation, the surgeon had to resort to hand-clamping various locations in an effort to determine the source of the blood flow. He couldn't see clearly through the vast amounts of blood and told me he had prayed for help. In his opinion, finding an aneurysm in a rare location like the splenetic artery was a miracle.

He went on to explain that the aneurysm had most likely been present in Matt's body since he was born, and just happened to rupture now. As I listened intently to his description of the surgery, I noticed a Star of David necklace below his shirt collar. Seeing this symbol of his faith encouraged me to say that I believed God had used him to save Matt's life. He humbly agreed and we marveled together at God's response to his prayer for help. Despite the differences in our religious backgrounds, we shared a common belief that God is present and that He listens to our prayers.

I was in awe when I realized that our family was the recipient of a miracle. The doctor's testimony validated my intuitive sense that God had moved in a very powerful way to save Matt's life. The ripple effects from this life-altering event would take years to unfold in both mine and Matt's lives; in different ways and at different times.

Many well-intentioned people told Matt that it wasn't his time to go and that God clearly had a plan for him. Although these statements were meant to reassure him, they seemed to weigh heavily on his mind as he pondered the fact that he was still alive. He told me that in the middle of the crisis, when he realized he might die, he prayed for his loved ones and then readied himself for the transition. When he came into awareness post-surgery, he felt a flood of mixed emotions. Sorting them out would take time and patience.

My experience of this miracle was, of course, different than Matt's, and he was fascinated to hear how events had unfolded for me. We were both filled with gratitude, as well as a sense of mystery and awe, upon realizing God's omnipresence. Humbled by His attention to the details of our ordinary lives, our faith grew by leaps and bounds during Matt's stay in the hospital.

As his condition improved, he was moved to a step-down unit for 10 days of careful monitoring while he recovered from his surgery. I remained in New Jersey during that time, sitting by his bedside during the day, and staying at his parent's house in the evenings. We arranged for his teenage son, Mickey, to travel by train from Virginia to visit. Matt also had many local visitors; cousins and family friends in the New Jersey area who wanted to see him. I found it stressful to be so far from home and I longed for the comfort and security of my own family. My brother Don called daily and provided a much needed sounding board as I processed aloud an overwhelming amount of medical information. On the weekend, he and his wife Maude traveled from New York City to visit us, as did my business partner Gary and his wife Marilyn. Their hugs, support, and sense of humor were reassuringly familiar to me.

Back in Maryland, Patrick and Ben were staying at the homes of two different friends, Tricia and Pat, during this time. I spoke to them by phone every day, but the separation was challenging for us all. The boys could not comprehend the magnitude of what had happened to their father and instead focused on the impact to their immediate world. They asked me why they couldn't be at their own home getting ready for Christmas like all of their friends were. The adults who were caring for them were kind and supportive, but our children missed us, as well as their home and normal routine.

During those weeks in the hospital, as I sat by Matt's bedside, my gaze would often fall on an empty chair on the other side of the room. I felt an energy coming from it and wondered what it was. I had plenty of hours to ponder what

I was experiencing, and in time, I realized that the energy I felt was Jesus. My earlier struggles to understand Him with my mind were somehow resolved now with an inner knowing of my heart and soul. I felt a tangible presence of God in human form in that empty chair.

My inner wisdom knew that God had provided for us every step of the way through this crisis. He had known what we would need even before we did, and He had provided for us through others. I was so very grateful for the love and support of the people in our lives. Cards flooded into Matt's room, and they covered an entire wall with well wishes from family and friends. Whenever we felt overwhelmed by the situation, we would re-read their messages and receive comfort and encouragement.

Matt had a few setbacks during his hospital stay, which prompted the doctors to order tests. One particular day, he underwent an eight-hour procedure. After drinking a prescribed fluid, he was taken by wheelchair to a laboratory in the far reaches of the hospital basement. Once the test was performed, we had to wait for the staff to wheel him back to his room. This pattern needed to be repeated several times throughout the day. In addition to the stress of Matt's impaired health, our situation was complicated by the fact that the nurses who worked at the hospital were on strike. As a result, many of the medical workers who were filling in for them were unfamiliar with the protocols of this particular facility.

After going back and forth between Matt's room and the basement four separate times, I noted how to navigate through the maze of hospital corridors. At one point, we waited patiently in the bowels of the basement for the transport to show up once again. Due to the staff shortage, it seemed to take forever for the attendant to arrive. Leaning against the drab basement wall, I observed Matt slouched in his wheelchair, shoulders hunched and watchfully waiting. Since the surgery, his eyes

> I felt a tangible presence of God in human form in that empty chair.

were wide and frightened much of the time. And no wonder; he had been through a shocking ordeal; experiencing a close brush with death and still unsure of what was coming next.

I grew tired of waiting for the transport and realized that I could find the way back to the room. Taking matters into my own hands, I pushed myself off the wall, grabbed the handles of Matt's wheelchair and said, "Hold on!" He looked at me in surprise and I nodded for him to take hold of his rolling IV pole, which we had named Harry in an effort to interject some humor into our situation. Matt's hands firmly grasped Harry and he positioned it in front of him as I took off down the hallway. Matt threw his head back and laughed out loud in sheer joy as we took charge of his life again. It was his first real laugh since coming back from death's door and I laughed along with him. By taking responsibility for what we could under the circumstances, we released some healing energy with our laughter. In that moment, we turned a corner, shook off victim mentality, and knew that we were going to survive this experience together.

Two weeks later, I took Matt home to his parent's house and then traveled back to Maryland to pick up our sons, who missed us desperately. I was so grateful for the friends who had cared for our children as if they were their own, while we dealt with the crisis-at-hand. The boys and I returned together to New Jersey and had a poignantly sweet Christmas with Matt, his parents, and his sister's family. Our time together was precious, given the experience we had just been through.

The following week, we returned home to Maryland and celebrated an especially meaningful New Year's Eve together. That evening, however, Matt spiked a fever and we went to the ER on New Year's Day. He had a post-operative infection and was admitted to the local hospital for care, where he spent another 10 days. His situation was not as critical as before, and I was able to be at home with our children at night and at the hospital during the day. The children and I celebrated Matt's 44th birthday with him in the hospital, surrounding him with our loving presence. He was less shell-shocked than before and was acutely grateful for the gift of life, despite another setback.

Once the immediate crisis subsided, I had time to reflect on all that had transpired. It's hard to put into words how deeply this entire experience impacted me. I had never been through a crisis of this magnitude, and was humbled at the realization that God had carried me through it. He provided everything I needed, and more. He took care of Matt. He took care of me. He took care of our children. He showed me, in a very real and tangible way, that I could count on Him. Everything I had ever learned about God up until this point had been preparing me to see Him in the empty chair in the hospital room and in the people He sent to help us. I knew on a deeper level that God is present in the daily details of life, whether in an ordinary day or in a crisis. I learned that God is personal and always with me. My responsibility is to remember to look for Him.

As significant as Matt's near-death experience had been for my faith, it was also an important turning point in our marriage. The two months that he spent recovering from surgery was the most emotionally and spiritually intimate time in our entire relationship. Despite being exhausted from caring for my family, while still maintaining my job, I was deeply happy in the newfound intimacy I had with God and with my husband.

This changed, however, when Matt returned to work. He chose to resume his familiar habits of smoking and drinking to deal with stress and to fill the spiritual void he felt inside. These habits had been a source of tension and arguments between us for years. I had hoped that his recent brush with death had transformed him, eradicating the tendency to overindulge, but I was wrong. I resented the return of the wedge between us that his drinking always created. I didn't know what to do with my anger, so I resorted to what I had always done; I stuffed it somewhere deep inside.

With Matt's health crisis over, I succumbed to exhaustion and despair, and entered a period of depression. I deeply felt the loss of my emotional connection with my husband, and sought guidance from the new associate pastor at my church. She told me that we all have to come down from the mountain top after intensely enlightening experiences. Just as the disciples wanted to build tents and stay on the mountain with Jesus after the Transfiguration when they realized who he was, my desires to keep the deep spiritual and emotional connections to Matt and God were not realistic. Disappointed and dissatisfied with her answer, and unsure of what to do next, I focused on the things that brought me fulfillment; my children, my friends, church, and my growing faith.

In the aftermath of this crisis, Matt and I struggled to find a new balance in our lives. In an effort to reconnect spiritually, we decided to attend the men's and women's 'Walk to Emmaus' weekends that our church was sponsoring later that spring. At the women's Emmaus weekend, my faith grew deeper still. Afterwards, Matt and I shared our experiences from these powerful retreats with one another. My hope for our marriage increased as we endeavored to deepen our relationship spiritually.

Even though we each had grown significantly in our faith, familiar unhealthy patterns of behavior resurfaced as life returned to normal. Matt sought solace and support at the local bar, while I diverted my frustration and anger into unrelenting busyness. We each found some comfort in these habitual coping mechanisms, but I knew on a deeper level that they were destroying the intimacy between us. Unable to change these ingrained tendencies, I overloaded my schedule with activity. A new and positive practice I created, however, was to pray and connect with God daily to nurture the tender shoot of personal faith that had sprouted so unexpectedly during this transformative time.

I wanted desperately to share my faith journey with Matt and continued to try to restore a connection with him. I knew, however, that no matter what path he chose to follow, I had to keep moving forward to a better understanding of my own relationship with God. The residual effects of that year were tremendous for me, and looking back, I can now see the directional changes that were set in motion.

Despite great efforts to reconcile, Matt and I had each made decisions that ultimately took us in separate directions. In time, I accepted that we grew as far as we could with one another. As heartbreaking as our divorce was, I had found a new and deeper connection with the Divine during our marriage, and I would treasure it forever. I know that God was then, and is now, present and available to me in a very personal way. I understand that my choices determine how close I feel to God and it's up to me to see Him at work in my life. Once I was on my own, I chose to continue on a spiritual path that led me to a deep and enduring bond with God unlike any other relationship in my life.

CHAPTER FOUR
REFLECTION QUESTIONS
Discovering Strength in Crisis

1. What challenges or crisis experiences have deepened your faith?

2. In what ways have you experienced God's presence during a challenging situation?

3. How did God provide for you before, during, and after that experience?

4. What changes did you make in your life as a result of this awareness?

5. What are the challenges of seeing God's provision for you in everyday life as opposed to His provision in times of great need?

CHAPTER *5*

Excavating Tels of
The Heart

Years after my divorce from Matt, I had the opportunity
to travel to Israel. While there, I saw a great variety
of tels. New to the world of Middle Eastern archeology,
I learned that a tel is a small elevation that marks the site of
an ancient city. As we approached Tel Hazor (pronounced
Hat-zor), the largest tel in Israel, my untrained eye saw just
another grassy hill in the rolling landscape of upper Galilee.
Our tour guide, Tsippi, escorted us to a wide, deep, hole in the
ground, where we could look down on carefully excavated
tiers of stones. I was surprised to see that hidden within
this hill were layers of history, dating back 4,000 years. I
saw remnants of walls that comprised the homes and public
spaces of what was once the largest fortified city in the time

of the Israelites. Located on the trade route between Egypt and Babylon in the days of David and Solomon, the Bible refers to Hazor as the head of all the kingdoms. In its day, it was ten times the size of Jerusalem.

Lifting my eyes and gazing at the peaceful fields surrounding Tel Hazor, I tried to picture the 20,000 people who experts estimate once lived there. In my mind's eye, I could see a bustling city filled with noise and confusion, as well as laughter and joy. I was aware that the intricacies of life happened on the very spot where I was standing, both the pleasant and unpleasant. People lived and died and each generation built walls to enclose their homes and the city itself. All that is left now are portions of those walls. Rocks, dust, and dirt remain to remind us of their story.

Examining the excavations, I could see exposed walls of houses, the palace, and the gated entrance to the city. Some of them actually dated back to the time of King Solomon and I marveled at how long these structures had stood stoically doing their job, well after their king and citizens had left the earth. Of course, now their purpose is no longer to safeguard the city, but to serve as a reminder of what once existed to those of us who visit this ancient site.

It occurred to me that I am like a tel. Buried within me are emotional walls that were formed for a reason. Although not nearly as old as the stones of Hazor, the inner walls around my heart were built layer upon layer for the purpose of self-protection. For many years, I was controlled by these concealed places. Hiding fearfully within these walls, I suffered alone, and believed I was the only one who had them. Now I understand that my behavior was not so unusual.

Although we all have unique life stories, most of us also share a common (and very human) habit of ignoring, denying, and doubting ourselves at times. Many of us have secret inner places where we hide and nurse the wounds that ultimately come with living our lives. Sometimes we are unaware of what we are concealing and why; other times we make a conscious choice to avoid something painful. We bury our fears so deeply because we are convinced that if they surfaced we would be overwhelmed. We simply don't allow ourselves to think about them. For many of us, it takes years to come face-to-face with the fears that lurk in our past. In spite of our best efforts to avoid them, they can cast long shadows over our hearts and minds and unknowingly drive our behaviors.

Understandably, most of us prefer to focus on pleasant memories. Happy recollections evoke positive energy and we willingly share them with others. Important lessons can be learned, however, from difficult situations. The treasures of self-acceptance and love are ours when we are willing to do the necessary work to become self-aware.

That being said, not all walls need to be excavated. In Israel, for example, there are tels that remain uncovered to this day. When questioned about them, Tsippi replied that the effort and cost involved in unearthing them would be too great. Our hearts can be like those tels. Sometimes we need to shine the light within our hidden areas to reveal (and heal) what lies there; other times we don't. Everything that we have lost doesn't necessarily have to be found. Whether or not we choose to do the inner work necessary to explore and understand the veiled areas of our hearts, we can still invite God inside. We don't have to be alone in our secret places. I believe that God wants to be there with us and to heal our wounds. If we decide to move forward and begin excavating an area of our hurting hearts, He will send helpers to guide our efforts.

A Buddhist proverb states, "When the student is ready, the teacher will appear." Every time that I have been ready to understand myself better, the right person has arrived to help me. These guides to greater wisdom have come in the form of friends, counselors, pastors, coaches, and sometimes even complete strangers who say or write words that impact me at just the right time. God has often worked through other people to heal my broken heart. And at times, He has simply abided patiently with me in my hidden place. He waits with loving arms until I am ready to give Him my pain and receive His healing. Whether or not I am aware of what lies concealed within me, He is able to wipe away my pain and suffering. My responsibility is to be willing to release it to Him, which is not always easy to do.

Just as ancient peoples knew to build walls to guard them from outside threats, I have instinctively known to protect myself from emotional danger. Relationships require a degree of vulnerability and risk that is very real. The potential for harm exists more often than I care to admit. Disappointment and emotional, mental, and physical pain are part of the human condition. The longer we live, the more we realize that good and bad co-exist and that life is filled with both positive and negative experiences.

The loss of trust is a potential result of hurtful occurrences. I learned to distrust assuming it was the most effective way to protect myself from further damage. With each injury, I added another stone of protection to the walls surrounding my heart.

> Everything that we have lost doesn't necessarily have to be found.

I would think to myself, *If that person hurt me once, he could do it again. I won't be so quick to trust him in the future.* Deep-seated fear led me to make a universal assumption; mistrusting all men because my husband and father had hurtfully let me down. Eventually, I realized that the fearful anticipation of being betrayed again was the reason I was safeguarding my heart.

Even after I recognized this habit of mistrust, it was still hard to remove. It has taken a conscious effort to replace my pattern of suspicion and cynicism with one of security and confidence.

I have grappled with difficult questions such as,

When someone lets me down, should I trust that person again, and how do I trust them?

When I trust someone who betrays me, was I wrong for trusting or was that person wrong for letting me down?

When I love someone who doesn't love me, am I a fool or a better person for having loved, even if that love wasn't returned?

Addressing these questions has helped me to develop new perspectives and begin breaking down my walls of distrust.

I saw that those fortifications only created an illusion of safety. In reality, they isolated me. Much like the Wizard of Oz concealed behind his curtain, I hid behind a façade, busily distracting attention elsewhere while hoping others wouldn't see the trembling girl within.

As I became aware of hiding, I questioned what purpose it was serving. I clearly felt that heart-protecting walls were necessary for my survival, but I also realized that no walls could shield me completely from the thoughtless and unsolicited actions of others (or even my unconscious self).

I felt the need for protection yet questioned the wisdom of allowing fear to be the foundation on which it was built. It seemed that when I allowed anxiety and doubt to be the driving forces behind self-protection, the walls grew inordinately large. I could see that some walls were necessary for healthy boundaries. However, it was challenging at first to determine the difference between a healthy boundary and an isolating, self-protective wall.

As I often remind my coaching clients, awareness creates choices. Applying this principle personally, I chose to courageously explore the nature of my walls to better understand them. This is an ongoing process. First, I assess their usefulness by asking myself if the original need for protection still exists. Finding the source of fear on which the wall is based, I evaluate whether it is serving me well or causing additional harm. With this insight, I can then take appropriate action either to accept or modify my self-protective walls.

As I did the inner excavation of the walls around my heart, I became aware of a dance that I do between fear, doubt, and trust. When I am fearful, my head disconnects from my heart and I forget to trust that God is present in my life. To reconnect my head and heart, I must lay down my fears and pick up faith instead. Trusting that He is guiding me and providing for my needs, I can release my anxious *what if* thinking and relax into His provision. This habit isn't easy for me and it takes continual practice to choose faith over fear.

I've learned that my anxieties grow larger when I don't trust others, myself, or God. Fears of being hurt, rejected, abandoned, and alone are at the core of our human experience. They are rooted in our need for security, love, and a sense of self-worth. These fears overlap one another and intertwine to such an extent that it is difficult to untangle and identify them individually. I have noticed, however, that several patterns emerged in my own life as I tried to manage the ripple effects of my apprehensions. Each pattern consisted of avoidance behaviors to protect me from fully experiencing difficult emotions that challenged me.

There are a variety of ways in which people avoid their fears; alcohol, drugs, food, shopping, work, sex, and busyness, to name just a few. Although I have indulged in many of these at one time or another, there are two patterns of avoidance that I consistently default to when I want to hide from stressors in my life.

My first go-to pattern to avoid intense or uncomfortable emotions resulting from anxiety or fear is to stay constantly busy. I overfill my life with so much activity that there isn't time to feel the unfamiliar and disquieting emotions that I want to avoid. I flop into bed exhausted each night after an excessively full day. I then find myself awake in the pre-dawn hours, mentally processing the worries and emotional baggage that I avoided during the previous day. When I'm using this avoidance pattern, I gain my sense of self-worth from what I accomplish each day. I feel validated as a worker, mother, and friend by what I *do* instead of by who I *am*. Letting my to-do list determine my value is short-sighted at best. When I am too busy, I don't take enough time to relax, laugh, or quietly be still. I sacrifice these important well-being ingredients and miss out on the joy, contentment, and peace that could be mine.

Fears, anxieties, and anger have a way of surfacing not only in the middle of the night but also in unexpected outbursts of either harsh words or tears. These flare-ups, as well as the restless nights, are red flags that something isn't right inside of me. It can take me awhile to pay attention to these warning signs in my life. Eventually, I am so exhausted by my hectic pace and from holding troubled emotions at bay that I give up on running away from whatever is bothering me. Noticing that my busyness is causing me to miss life's precious moments and beauty, I remind myself that I want to lead a calm, peaceful, and grounded life. This means I have to face the fears and anxieties that challenge me, work through them, and when I am ready, release them.

My second avoidance pattern, which I have repeated for years, is one of over-connecting and disconnecting with significant people in my life. Unlike the first pattern, in which I try to gain my sense of self-worth and value from what I *do*, in this pattern I try to attain it from my relationships with others. At first, I want to be close and I allow others to become significant in my life. It shifts out of balance, however, when I put them on a pedestal and allow their opinion of me to matter more than my own. I compare myself to others and think I do not measure up. I get caught up in thinking that I am not smart enough, pretty enough, or good enough. I give my personal power away and become dependent on others to feel good about myself. This leads to being anxiously attached and needy. I become overwhelmed by my neediness and then disconnect emotionally to rebalance. At first, this disconnection feels safe but eventually it leads to feelings of isolation and loneliness. Being too close or too alone are red flags telling me that I am struggling to find equilibrium in relationships.

Fear of intimacy has produced invisible walls that disengage me from myself, God, and others. It is uncomfortable to be vulnerable enough to be truly close. I want that intimacy yet I fear losing myself. I know that focusing on others prevents me from connecting to my own heart and the spirit of God within me. As the line in a country song says, "I'm looking for love in all the wrong places" by attempting to find a connection with my true inner self through my relationships with other people. When I fall into this avoidance pattern, I forget the importance of loving myself and trusting God with all that concerns me.

While these are my two primary avoidance patterns, I have combined them with others in my efforts to escape painful feelings. To be honest, at times I have run from one avoidance behavior to another, desperately trying to find a place where there is the least amount of anxiety and fear. The truth is that the only place such peace exists is in my relationship with God. What can I do when my heart needs security? If I look for it outside of myself, in other relationships, activities, material possessions, appearances, career, finances, or other worldly things, it eventually leads to disappointment.

Over time, I have learned to lean on my faith and prayerfully take my requests and fears to God, so that I can release them. Humans may not always be trustworthy, but God is. I rely on Him more and more and reap the benefits of a contented and peaceful heart. I have felt empowered to change as I put my trust in God and let go of overwhelming fear.

However, just as some of the tels in Israel remain unearthed, I was relieved when experts informed me that I don't have to remember the details of my own personal history in order to heal. Abuse that I suffered as a child is one of my tels that would be too costly for me to fully excavate. It would take too great a toll to explore. Like the stones in the ancient walls hidden beneath the ground, my heart history lies within me, providing a structure on which I build my current life. Knowing the self-protective walls are there, it is up to me to decide which tels of my heart need to be excavated. By identifying my fears and any unhealthy avoidance patterns that exist, I have the opportunity to let them go. I prayerfully give them to God and release them into His care. This sets me free to live a life where I am close to others physically, emotionally, and spiritually; trusting whole-hearted connections in healthy relationships.

Examining my self-protective walls and the fears they have been built upon, has helped me learn to gently love and accept myself. This, in turn, has given me a greater ability to compassionately love and accept others. In hindsight, I understand why, and how, my walls initially developed. Equipped with this information, the choices before me are revealed. I can modify the walls, deconstruct them altogether, or simply ask God to heal and remove them for my optimal health and well-being.

CHAPTER FIVE
REFLECTION QUESTIONS

Discovering Your Heart

1. What self-protective walls have you put around your heart to safeguard it?

2. What are your typical avoidance patterns?

3. In what ways could God provide some of the emotional protection and security that your heart needs?

4. "When we learn to love and accept ourselves, we are better able to love and accept others." What do you believe about this statement?

CHAPTER *6*

Walls of My Heart

For much of my life, I didn't even know I was building walls around my heart. I was oblivious to their existence until I began to question the part that I played in my failing marriage. As I observed the ways in which I distanced myself from others, and admitted the problems that this behavior created in my relationship with Matt, I began to question my motivation.

Like many people, my avoidance behaviors developed as a result of experiences in childhood. I put self-protective walls around my heart when I was sexually abused by a distant relative at a very young age. I locked up the awful memories and essentially threw away the key. My knowledge of the abuse remained buried deep inside of me; I had absolutely no recollection of it until it unexpectedly surfaced when I was in my mid-forties. Like stones within a tel, my suppressed memories provided a framework on which many of my behaviors were based. I was unaware of the impact that this repressed experience had upon me while I was growing up.

I adopted several questionable limiting beliefs in order to cope with my experiences. One such belief was *People will only like me if I am quiet and compliant.* Consequently, I didn't speak up and was perceived as a shy, yet helpful, child. In reality, I was a people-pleaser who didn't have the confidence to use her voice.

Another belief I adopted was *Don't draw attention to yourself.* I was dreadfully afraid of being the center of attention and would blush bright red when I thought all eyes were on me. I was most comfortable when I could melt into a group of people and go unnoticed. I liked being invisible yet also struggled with it. I grew up trying to assimilate mixed messages such as *Be pretty, but not too pretty. Be smart, but not too smart. Play small and let others think they are smarter, prettier, and better than you.* The goal was to minimize myself in an effort to avoid being noticed. Confused and bewildered, I sought to avoid my inner turmoil by finding my purpose and value in my relationships with others.

By the age of seven, I began my relationship avoidance pattern when I found an escape in the role of 'mother's helper'. I regularly took care of my youngest brother, Andrew, and my sister, Ellen, whom I called 'my babies'. Caring for them was a way to steer clear of my own pain. Being a middle child in a large family provided a natural environment for me to hide and be small. My helpfulness was appreciated and reinforced by my mother. I wanted to be a good girl at home and at school. The ways in which I managed to cope were socially acceptable, so the adults in my life thought I was fine. They perceived me as being easy-going.

My avoidance patterns expanded, however, when I entered my teens. I indulged in the sex, drugs, and rock-n-roll culture of the late 1970s. I chose to avoid emotional pain by surrounding myself with a rowdy crowd who liked to party. The walls around my heart became thicker and higher as I stacked one poor choice on top of another, losing myself in confusion and suffering. Within my group of friends I felt normal, and I tried to reassure myself that I was fine. I reasoned that I wasn't so bad; after all, there were others who were wilder than me. I had my limits and I didn't go beyond them. However, I never stopped to think whether those self-imposed limits were healthy or not.

I also never asked myself what really drove me to do the things I did. Some actions I can attribute to being young and feeling invincible. Beyond that, however, there was an undercurrent of constant fear that was driving my behavior. I sought pleasure and short-term gratification in an effort to ignore the fact that I couldn't trust myself or the significant men in my life. My walls were solid and my fears compelled me to continue building them higher to avoid an unconscious inner pain. I would have periodic moments of awareness in which I would make clear and healthy choices, but these were infrequent. When I was 15 years old, I fell in love with a boy who was three years older than I was, much to my parents concern. I tried to fill my hurting heart and soul with an emotional and physical connection that I was too young to fully comprehend.

My avoidance patterns of partying and co-dependent relationships continued into my college years. After my first semester in New Hampshire, I was shocked to learn that my parents were separating due to an affair that my father was having with his secretary. In the tumultuous months that then led to their divorce, I sometimes felt caught in the middle of their unraveling relationship. Mom relied on us older children for support while Dad proceeded to move on and start another phase of life with a new wife and her children. It was an extremely emotional time and, as is often the case with divorce, hurtful things were said which left lasting scars.

Unaware of the complex forces that were driving my father's decisions, I pleaded with him not to leave the family. Looking back on that confrontation, I now realize that he may have felt that he was backed into a corner with no winning solution in sight. Consequently he angrily declared that he was divorcing his children along with their mother. At 18 years of age he insisted that I no longer needed him. It was an emotionally charged conversation and I was deeply hurt and profoundly angry over his perceived rejection. He remained financially responsible but significantly less available to me in the years that followed. Having no skills to deal with such powerful emotions, I buried them deep inside with my other unresolved wounds.

For the remainder of my college years, I continued my avoidance behaviors of partying and overly focusing on others. After I graduated, I began to work full time and this lifestyle change dictated that I settle down a bit. I limited my indulgences to the weekends. Two years after graduating, I fell in love and became engaged to Matt, and discovered even more ways to focus my energy on others.

Matt and his young son became the center of my world, a world that still included a significant amount of partying. A big shift occurred, however, two years into our marriage when I became pregnant. I immediately stopped drinking, making a conscious choice to protect my unborn child.

Being a mother became the most important thing in my life. I avoided my inner pain by caring for my family and arranged to work from home to be present with my new son Patrick. I became a consummate juggler of household, children, marriage, church, and career. My organizational skills were lauded by employers and volunteer leaders who encouraged me to give, and give, and give some more. By now, I had effectively replaced partying with busyness. I valued being productive and forgot how to relax and be at ease. There was always something that needed to be done, and I did it. Even though I had significantly changed my partying habits by this time, Matt chose to continue drinking and it became a source of conflict between us.

By my mid-thirties, my inner walls were firmly established. I conducted my life with organizational skill and finesse. I found great pleasure in providing a happy childhood for our children, who were the center of my world. They were well-behaved (for the most part) and our home was filled with a great deal of joy, laughter, and exuberance. I successfully balanced parenting and volunteering with running a home-based business and from the outside, everything looked fine.

My foundation was rocked, however, four years after Matt had his aneurysm. While doing laundry one day, I discovered a love letter in his pocket from a co-worker and was shocked to learn that he was having an affair. I felt completely blindsided. Never in my wildest dreams could I have ever anticipated such a betrayal from this man whom I loved and had been through so much with. I reached a new level of despair in the months following this discovery. I was shaken to my core, realizing that the bubble I had been living in had burst. I could no longer put on a happy face and pretend that we were a functional family. Matt and I immediately sought the help of professional counselors as we struggled to understand what this meant to our relationship.

My buried feelings about the abuse I had suffered as a child and my father's emotional abandonment after divorcing my mother had silently, yet powerfully, compounded within me. Matt's infidelity was the last straw that sent me over a mental and emotional edge. My lowest point came after yet another searing argument with Matt. Frustrated, furious, and deeply hurt, I walked out the door on a bitter cold January night. I was distraught and crying, and didn't know where I was going. I just had to get away. I had a vague idea that I would walk to my friend Pat's house and headed in that general direction, not thinking about the eight miles of fields and streams that I would have to traverse in the dark. Walking through my neighborhood in tears, I came to the end of a court and stood before an empty field.

It was early in the evening and the velvety sky was dark with crystal-like stars that sparkled above me. The field was white with snow and I could see my breath as I began to tromp over the brambles and brush poking out of the white mounds. My feet broke through the crusty surface layer of snow and sank into the soft powder below. I slowed my pace and turned my heartfelt crying to God. My emotions swept over me and I felt utterly lost. I lay down in the field and wept my heartache into the cold ground. The entire structure of my life, and everything that I believed in, had been shaken. Exhausted from trying to hold my marriage together for years, I now succumbed to complete despair.

Even in the midst of my agony that night, however, I knew that God was my constant companion. I prayed to be taken out of this painful place where my heart was breaking with the betrayal of misguided love. In that dark moment, I didn't want to live; my misery was so deep and I cried for God to take me away from it. I don't know how long I laid there in the snow, but it was long enough to chill me to the bone.

Eventually, I was roused from my sobbing by the sound of an engine growing louder. Alarmed, I poked my head up like a groundhog from its hole to see a snowmobile heading directly towards me. The whine of its engine grew louder as its headlight bobbed across the white field in my direction. I believe that God will use any way possible to reach us in our times of desolation, and on that particular night, He used a stranger on a snowmobile to startle me out of my anguished pit. I don't know if it was vanity or a survival instinct, but I sat up and pulled myself together, not wanting the rider to drive over me; for his sake as well as mine. I stood up and stumbled away, still praying to God for deliverance from my emotional pain.

My desperate thoughts were replaced with a desire to flee and avoid having to explain my odd behavior to someone I didn't know. Wandering aimlessly at first, I began to feel an invisible cord pulling me forward. It came directly out of my center as if it was an umbilical cord. I didn't know what was on the other end, but I allowed it to pull my numb mind and body forward. I let the invisible cord pull me through the streets of my neighborhood and eventually realized it was drawing me home.

Soon after, I found myself stumbling through the side door of our house. The warmth of the room hit me like a sauna and I collapsed to the floor. Matt was beside himself with worry, having no idea where I had gone in my distressed state. He had fervently prayed for my safe return. Later, as I soaked in a tepid tub to slowly warm my body temperature, I realized that God was with me in the darkest night of my life. He had used the very person who betrayed me, along with a snowmobile angel, to bring me back from the edge of despair. I saw a small glimmer of hope that all was not lost. God found me in that field and I knew that He would stay with me through the turmoil ahead.

As I recovered from that difficult night, I started to ask myself two simple yet powerful questions: *What was my part in all of this?* and *What did I do—or not do— to contribute to us getting to this point in our relationship?* I believe that a marriage is a 50/50 partnership, so I wanted to know what went wrong in my half.

Marriage counseling was helpful and started a long journey of healing for me. The counselor wisely recommended that Matt and I also meet individually with him. During one of these sessions I had a moment of awakening when he asked me a simple question, "What do *you* need?" I was dumbfounded to realize that I had absolutely no idea how to answer him. I knew what everyone close to me needed, and I actively sought to meet those needs, but I didn't know what *I* needed. With dawning awareness I realized that I was an expert on the needs of others, yet knew very little about myself. I pictured myself as a ghost; an indistinct figure lacking clear definition.

Transparent and barely there, I routinely put myself at the bottom of my own list. I focused on service and on most days time ran out before I got around to my needs. With this new awareness I gradually started to learn how to take time for myself along with all of the other people and activities that I cared about. It started with simply giving myself permission to stop for a cup of coffee as I ran errands for others. This felt indulgent at first and I struggled with the perception that it was selfish to take care of my own needs, but I made myself persevere with this new practice. The concept of self-care was unfamiliar and I wrestled with the belief that others would judge or reject me if I practiced it. I progressed from cups of coffee to reading a book for pleasure or having lunch with a friend. I learned how to ask myself what I needed and to answer that need whenever possible. As I did this, I started to gradually depend less on others for my happiness and more on myself. I began to create an identity that wasn't based on how others perceived or judged me, but that came from an internal source of love and acceptance.

With the help of counseling and prayer, I started to work on identifying the inner walls that had been hidden by a façade of respectability and competence. In *Matthew 7:7*, Jesus said, "Ask, and it will be given to you; seek and you will find, knock and it will be opened to you." Believing the promise of those words, and feeling hopeful, I embarked on an inward journey to know myself better and to seek healing for my broken heart.

For the first time in my life, I spent countless hours in therapy, and courageously explored untapped areas of my past. I came to understand that alcoholism was in my family of origin and that my marriage had similar problems. I began to discern what was and wasn't my part in regard to these issues.

At the suggestion of several people, I eventually gathered the courage to go to an Al-Anon meeting. I didn't know what to expect but hoped that this resource for people in relationships with alcoholics would prove helpful. I was pleasantly

> I learned how to ask myself what I needed and to answer that need whenever possible.

surprised to learn of its spiritual approach and became a regular attendee at meetings. Al-Anon taught me The Serenity Prayer and I repeated it frequently:

> *God grant me the serenity to accept the things I cannot change; the courage to change the things I can; and the wisdom to know the difference.*

It provided a framework for me as I tried to differentiate myself from others. I learned how to assume responsibility for myself and to realize that this was not selfish. I began to understand the ramifications of my behavior when I got into other people's business in an effort to avoid my own pain and suffering.

In the recovery community, I made new friendships that supported my growth and self-discovery. Although I was in a pit of despair, I imagined looking up and seeing those who cared for me sitting around the edge. They did not climb into the pit with me but were keeping me company, providing reassurance that I was not alone during those dark times. I drew great comfort from their presence while I continued to seek a way out of the self-destructive habits that I had relied on for so long.

I believe that God doesn't intend for us to go through life alone. Fortunately, I have been blessed with many incredible women in my life; a beloved mother, two wonderful sisters, a dear cousin, sisters-in-law, and many precious friends who I value as sisters-of-the-heart. Their patience was no doubt tested at times by the long conversations we would have, during which I would process aloud my thoughts and emotions. As I untangled my anxious attachment to Matt and my frenzied avoidance of pain through busyness, I relied on their wise counsel and even more on their patient and reflective listening. These were gifts freely given by them, communicating messages of love, acceptance, and faithful companionship that had a deep impact. These women played a crucial role as I sought to discover my own inner wisdom—my wise self.

As I chose to lean on others, including my family, friends, pastor, and counselors, I created a team that helped me climb out of my pit. In addition to attending Al-Anon meetings,

I joined classes to learn meditation, yoga, and other techniques to center myself and bring peace and harmony to my life. Using these methods regularly, I constructed a virtual ladder out of the pit of my confusion and despair. I opened my mind to new teachers and read many books by the Buddhist monks Thich Nhat Hanh and Pema Chodron. I learned about loving kindness and tried to treat myself with the same care that I would offer to a dear friend. I began to practice mindfulness to slow down and better appreciate life. It felt unfamiliar to be so focused, yet the end result was incredibly calming. I attempted to eat, walk, and sit mindfully, trying to be fully present in the moment. My efforts were supported in this endeavor when I joined a local community that met weekly to meditate together. The leader would share inspirational readings such as the poetry of Rumi or lead us in kirtan, an ancient type of call-and-response chanting. These experiences were new and somewhat uncomfortable, yet they filled me with an inner peace that I had never known before.

What started as a thought grew into a way of being as I integrated these new customs into my lifestyle. I made friends in the community who became fellow journeyers in the search for healing and personal enlightenment. In group therapy, I talked about topics that were challenging for me and practiced being vulnerable with others. I developed a trusting bond with the women in the group, many of whom also became dear sisters-of-the-heart. Each person, program, and practice was a vital rung of the ladder that eventually led to my recovery.

Being open to learning new things was crucial to my success. Practicing meditation and yoga helped me slow down and be present in the moment, if only for a few minutes at a time. I started to feel peace through these practices as I learned to detach from my thoughts and let myself just *be*. I cultivated my ability to simultaneously focus on an image, or hold a pose, while releasing thoughts that distracted and concerned me. I imagined that my thoughts were a babbling brook, and that I was sitting on the grassy riverbank, watching them flow by. Learning how to detach from my thoughts was a skill with great rewards. Not only did it bring a sense of calm to my spirit that I had longed for my whole life, it allowed me to experience a peaceful inner place where I was pleasantly surprised to find God. These practices not only improved my physical and mental well-being, but my spiritual connection as well.

Taking aerobic and yoga classes helped me to feel more comfortable in my own skin. Whether I was pushing myself aerobically or stretching and holding poses while breathing mindfully, I was reconnecting to my body.

———————————

And so it happened that I was in the child pose of yoga at home one day when the abuse memories of my childhood finally burst through the walls and surfaced. I had buried them so deeply that I couldn't recognize the powerful emotions that were pouring out of me. My gut instinct was to curl up in the fetal position and allow myself to sob and discharge my pent up emotions. The intensity of the release frightened me, and once the experience subsided, I immediately called my counselor.

He explained that repressed memories will arise when we are able to handle and process them. The fact that mine had emerged at this time was an indicator that my inner self felt safe enough to let them out. Although it was a surprise that I had kept such powerful information buried inside me for so many years, I was not in disbelief of the revelation. In fact, I had an inner knowing of the truth and in many ways the knowledge of it resolved questions that were unanswered from my past. Like a puzzle piece finally fitting into place, I came to understand many things about myself; my insecurity and lack of trust being two of the most important revelations. With the help of my counselor and the validation of some family members, I came to understand and eventually accept that I had been sexually abused as a baby by a distant relative. That early trauma had impacted my growth throughout my life. Unable to trust myself or others to protect me, I had adopted ways to cope with this experience, which helped me to exist in the world.

Even with the progress I was making through counseling and other healthy practices, I found it difficult to speak to others about my experiences with alcoholism and abuse.

A sense of shame overpowered me and initially I didn't share these challenges with anyone other than my trusted inner circle. I was deeply embarrassed by our family's issues and struggled to deal with the complexity of alcoholism, co-dependency, and infidelity. In addition, I had no idea what to make of the repressed abuse memories. It was especially difficult to continue participating in the church community that I had shared with Matt. The dissolution of my world left me confused about my own identity and I needed a safe place to retreat where no one knew me or expected anything of me.

I decided to start attending another church closer to my home where I could worship anonymously and be comforted by God's presence there. Fortuitously, this nearby church had just begun a contemporary service and I discovered that I thoroughly enjoyed this new style of worship. The repetitive nature of the upbeat music was almost meditative as the rhythm and words settled into my receptive heart. The straightforward and meaningful messages of the pastors touched me and lifted my spirit, providing comfort and acceptance at a time when I was working my way through a tangled web of emotions.

This new church community provided a secure place to sing, pray, and sometimes weep as I tried to make sense of my crumbling world. Free of any church responsibilities other than to attend worship, I found it easier to connect to God in this new community. My hurting soul was comforted as I received the blessed acceptance of these strangers.

In time, I learned that the walls that I had constructed over my entire life were put in place unconsciously by me as protection from further suffering. As I grew up, these walls remained in place long after they were needed and now only served to hold in the pain. When my marriage fell apart, I crumbled in an emotional heap, exhausted from trying to hold it all together for so long. The large-and-in-charge Carol started to become more vulnerable. Seeing that my existing methods weren't working, I became willing to let others inside my head and heart to help me sort through my troubled perspectives. I continued to pray, read inspirational books, and write in my journal in order to capture and process my thoughts and feelings.

I admitted that I didn't have it all together and humbly sought God. I asked for His help to mend my hurting heart. Like the crippled woman who had been bent over for 18 years *(Luke 13:10-13)*, I chose to approach Jesus with my troubles, believing He could heal me. It seemed as though I had to hit rock bottom before I could surrender my will to God and allow Him to begin His healing work within me. It wasn't until I admitted that I couldn't do it on my own, and needed help, that things really began to change.

The inward journey to heal the wounds from my past has taken many years and will subtly continue throughout my life. In time, I have learned that the people who inadvertently caused me harm were, in fact, catalysts for my growth into the woman I am today. I wouldn't be who I am now without the heartache and trials I have been through, and for that I am grateful. As I sought to understand and forgive my father and my husband, I came to see that they each loved me very much and did not intend to hurt me with their words or actions. They were each most likely doing the best they could at very difficult times in their own lives.

Poignantly, my father and I were able to begin repairing our relationship six months prior to his unexpected death. With counseling, I released my anger towards him and rediscovered my love and appreciation for him as that self-protective wall crumbled. The healing of my relationship with my father is on-going. Some of this healing occurred during the writing of this book twenty-three years after his death when my siblings and I had the opportunity to share our unique perspectives about him with one another. Acknowledging the powerful figure he was to each of us has led me to further embrace the many gifts he gave to me.

My husband Matt and I, after years of trying to mend our relationship, sadly determined that our marriage was irreconcilable, and we went our separate ways. The process of forgiveness continues with him as well, as we each have taken our lives in new directions.

———

It was during the difficult years of separation and divorce that I started to understand the nature of the protective walls around my heart and the fears on which they were based. I identified my anxieties and saw how they motivated me to create emotional distance in order to feel safe, yet they also isolated me. Although each concern, like stones in an actual wall, was different, they were really all the same in the end. At their root, they were all created by some form of fear.

The fear of being hurt again manifested itself in my romantic relationships following my divorce. To avoid the risk of being betrayed and devastated once more, I kept an emotional distance with the men I dated. I just wanted to have fun, and wasn't interested in a serious relationship or a second marriage. I didn't want to risk losing myself in another relationship. Some of this desire for detachment was based on experiences with my father and husband, which had led me to conclude that men, in general, were not trustworthy. Even though my head knew that wasn't true of all men, my heart wasn't willing to take the risk of getting romantically close again.

Not trusting myself to maintain healthy boundaries in romance, I limited my dating and chose instead to focus my energy on raising my sons while expanding my business. Fortunately, I enjoyed healthy relationships with my three brothers, my sons, my beloved uncle, and my male cousins. I gratefully appreciated their presence in my life and the reassurance they provided that all men weren't hurtful.

I struggled with other fears as well, and they often conflicted with one another, trapping my head in a swirl of confusion. My emotional walls gave me the illusion of security. It was difficult to challenge the habits that were designed to make me feel safe and comfortable. However, I knew that I needed to do so if I were to finally be free of the walls and the emotional distance they ensured. This was necessary in order to achieve the deeper and more intimate connection that I desired with myself, others, and God.

The fear of being alone and going through life unloved, was juxtaposed by the fear of being close and intimate. My longing for love was counterbalanced by a deep fear of (and inexperience with) genuine emotional, physical, and spiritual intimacy.

I feared slowing down since it meant that I would feel more of my emotional pain. I wanted to eliminate my avoidance habit of busyness because I knew my constant activity was preventing me from enjoying the precious moments of my life. I wanted to stop being so busy, yet slowing down and being still in order to savor life, and connect with myself and God, meant that I would feel my heartache.

I was also fearful of failing but at the same time, was anxious about succeeding. I wanted success but was concerned about the impact it would have on my current life balance. Patterns of failure, though unhealthy, were at least familiar, and I mindlessly repeated them until I was challenged by new ways of thinking. I believed that if I stayed small and invisible, people would not expect much from me. I reasoned that I couldn't disappoint others (or myself) if I didn't try.

Comparing myself with others, I often fell short of my own expectations and gave into the fear of rejection. Thinking others wouldn't understand, like, or accept me; I protectively kept to myself and didn't risk being known. Whether I deemed myself better or worse than others, it brought about the same result: distance. Labeling myself as different was a protective shield that I could hide behind and feel safe.

I learned many ways to disconnect my heart from others in my efforts to keep it protected. At the core was a belief that if I were to completely be myself, others wouldn't love me. I believed a foundational message that it was not okay, or safe, to be who I was. As I converged on my fears, my anxieties grew. I fell back on my habits of staying busy and focusing my attention on others to help me manage the overwhelming work of facing my neurotic tendencies. Ultimately, it was a process that took a great deal of patience and loving-kindness.

Even as I challenged existing walls, I developed new fears and found it necessary to create fresh walls to protect myself. During my marital separation, I created new boundaries and habits; some healthy and some not. Early on, I discovered that I was terrified of being alone. When my sons would spend the weekend with their father, I felt lost and unsure of what to do without the responsibilities of being a mom. It felt strange to be in the house alone and I fearfully locked the doors, compulsively checking and rechecking them in an effort to feel safe. Still harboring a lot of anger, I bordered on being paranoid, like a child fearfully thinking the boogie-man was lurking behind closed doors.

With perseverance and hard work, I overcame this anxiety and learned to enjoy my solitude. I came to see these times on my own as an opportunity to take care of myself and enjoy activities that I had let go of in my single-minded focus on pleasing others.

There were times, however, when my peaceful aloneness turned into loneliness and I came to realize that I needed to deconstruct the protective walls that isolated me. One step at a time, I identified and released my fears, becoming more self-aware and letting the light stream into the dark corners of my heart. The places I had kept hidden were gradually illuminated as I began to know and trust myself. Letting go of fear and replacing it with God's love and grace on a daily basis, my heart and spirit grew stronger. I learned to love the unique creation that God had made me to be.

Eventually, I felt called to share the wisdom that I had discovered. I started to use the talents that God had given me and the life experiences I had been through to encourage others in their spiritual and personal growth. I began teaching Sunday school and continued to do so for many years, guiding youth as they questioned, discussed, and accepted their own relationships with God. I discovered a love for helping people to develop; leading them to a-ha moments when they gained insights that were personally relevant to them. Experiencing success in this area, I gradually overcame my desire to be invisible. I realized that I wanted to show up in life and serve God with the talents that I uniquely possessed. This led me back to school to become an accredited coach, where I honed my abilities to guide myself and others towards greater consciousness and fulfillment.

I had come a long way. Enjoying this new phase of life, I arose each day feeling energized, expressive, and rich in a life abundant with the love of family and friends. I fell asleep at night feeling grateful for the experiences each day had brought. Yet, even with this contentment, I still felt that something was missing from my life. In the quiet morning hours, when I would come into wakefulness, I was aware of a certain sadness. A quiet crying of my heart was present, which alerted me to the unrest in my soul. There was an inner child in me who longed for comfort, love, and care. In those early morning hours, I knew I had more healing to do. The walls needed to come all the way down, so I embarked on a journey to continue to heal my broken heart.

For years, I had been chipping away at the stones in my walls like a mason with a hammer and they were crumbling slowly. Occasionally, I redefined a wall into a healthy boundary or inadvertently built new ones as I discovered fresh fears. I now knew how to identify, assess, and deconstruct the unnecessary ones more quickly than in the past. I had become skillful at self-awareness and was able to help others move forward in their own search for higher consciousness. I continued the daily practices of prayer and meditation to connect with God, seeking His grace and mercy in my life. I was consistently open to a relationship with a Power greater than myself and strove to trust God more and more. Eventually, I invited Him into my buried memories to transform me and remove any remnants of pain. Ultimately, despite all of my own efforts, there were some walls inside of me that only He could remove. After years of learning and acquiring tools for self-development, I was sufficiently open and trusting for God to heal my heart swiftly, silently, and unexpectedly… which He did in three profound experiences that were to come.

CHAPTER SIX
REFLECTION QUESTIONS

Discovering Support and Self-Care

1. What are you afraid of?

2. What supports you during fearful times?

3. What do you believe about the perspective that God will use any means possible to reach us in our times of desolation; such as a stranger riding a snowmobile on a snowy night?

4. In what ways have you created a network of support to get you through difficult times? What resources have you used, or would you like to use, in the future?

5. What do you do to take care of yourself?

6. How necessary is self-care to your well being?

7. What helps you to overcome any beliefs you may have that self-care is selfish?

8. Being open and willing to change is a key characteristic of growth. In what ways are you currently open to change?

9. What practices connect you to your heart and soul?

CHAPTER *7*

Healings of the Heart

My three heart healings occurred in unexpected places as I opened myself to learning about other spiritual practices and religions. The first healing was set in motion when I accepted an invitation from my massage therapist to visit the local Sufi community. I was curious to attend their worship service and see what I could learn about this branch of the Islam religion. Entering the large old house where they gathered, I left my shoes by the door and joined the others who sat on the floor in a large circle. As a woman, I was expected to cover my head, and a scarf was provided. Even though the request was unusual to me, I was eager to fit in and willingly complied. I draped a scarf over my head as I settled myself on a cushion, observing the friendly faces that welcomed me. The leader, Salima, was a small woman with a warm smile. She read from a book of Sufi teachings called *Music of the Soul** and spoke words of inspiration and love. She then led us in a rhythmic chant, which I found both unusual and uplifting. Like all Muslims, Sufis refer to God as Allah. This custom was unfamiliar to me; however, I found that the similarities in our beliefs far outweighed the differences. The universal message of love was present whenever I worshipped with them; and I chose to do so regularly. I was given the Sufi name Rahima, which means "one whose heart is filled with the mercy from God." I attended several day-long workshops to deepen my understanding of their religion and to grow personally.

In time, I learned that Salima was also a healer. Although small in stature, she had a surprisingly powerful impact on others. She seemed to have a sixth sense, and radiated a calm and accepting energy. Her long brown hair and warm compassionate eyes seemed to see right into the heart of those she encountered, embracing them with loving kindness. I enjoyed being around her, as did many others who soaked in her healing energy. She blessed and nurtured the Sufi community in our area with her wisdom and grace.

Even though we had different religious beliefs, I connected with Salima on a universally spiritual level. I felt

---

**Music of the Soul: Sufi Teachings, Shaykh Muhammad Sa'id al-Jamal ar-Rifa'i as-Shadhuli, Sidi Muhammad Press, Petaluma, CA, 2002.*

God's presence when I prayed with the community and knew He was with us in a very tangible way. I felt out of my comfort zone each time I visited the Sufi community, yet I returned again and again because I was drawn to the kind, healing energy they offered. I sensed that they had something I needed. I was curious about the universal essence of God that I experienced with these people who called Him by different names and read about Him in different texts. I practiced a meditative ritual of saying Allah in two syllables (Ah-*lah*), as the second syllable rolled off my tongue with an expulsion of breath. Salima taught us that the 'Ah' sound

The universal message of love was present.

opens not only our mouths but our hearts as well. I felt my heart and soul open with the repetition of this holy name of God expressed over and over again. The soft breathy quality of the word was a prayer in itself.

The Sufi community taught me how to say Jesus in Arabic: *Isa* (pronounced *eessa*). I found it incredibly comforting to fill my lungs with the swirling breaths of these holy names for God. I began to use them whenever I would awaken in the middle of the night with anxiety in my heart and fearful thoughts. Repeating them over and over again like a mantra, my breaths would fill my lungs, and God's presence would seep into my mind and body until I drifted back to sleep. Despite the differences in our habits, there was a universal commonality in our beliefs, and I experienced the comfort of God's presence when I was with this community of believers.

After spending several months visiting the Sufi community, I decided to meet with Salima for private healing sessions. I was surprised at her intuitive ability and healing touch. As I grew to trust her, I accepted her invitation to attend a four-day intensive healing retreat, at which I could focus specifically on my childhood abuse issues. I wasn't sure what to expect but tried to enter with an open mind to see what would happen. Days of eating simple, healthy food, meditating frequently, and taking advantage of services such as zero balancing and cranio-sacral work left me feeling relaxed and receptive. That is when the unexpected occurred and I experienced a profound emotional healing.

During a private meditative session, I unexpectedly had an out-of-body experience during which I observed the abuse that happened to me as a baby. I felt great distress and a strong desire to get away. Overcome with fear and anxiety, I was aware of a protective energy entering the room. Initially, it was my paternal grandmother's reassuring presence that brought immediate relief. However, God then entered my vision, picked up my small body, and carried me away from the painful circumstance. In swift and silent motions, He lifted me out of that situation forever. Tearful and exhausted, I felt a great release and knew in my core that something harmful had been taken away from me. I was freed from the pain of that memory. Later, I was relieved to hear Salima explain that it isn't necessary to remember or relive a traumatic experience in order to be healed from it.

———————

My second emotional healing occurred years later, again unexpectedly. A week prior to the occurrence of this healing, I had attended a three-day workshop called *Healing the Courageous Heart* through the Personal Transformation and Courage Institute in Virginia. During this workshop, I learned that wounded and broken hearts are a universal experience. I began to gently and lovingly embrace the strength and vulnerability of my own wounded heart and specifically focused on understanding my inner child. Through experiential exercises, we learned to transform our pain to access the strength and courage within our own hearts. I purposefully focused on creating new connections with the frightened little girl inside of me. The workshop left me feeling incredibly open and receptive and soon after I experienced a second profound healing of my heart.

Within a week of attending the workshop, I was traveling with my friend Linda when we passed The National Shrine Grotto of Lourdes, which is next to the campus of Mount St. Mary's University in Emmitsburg, MD. This replica of the Grotto of Lourdes in France was a special place for Linda because she had donated a stone bench there in memory of her late mother. In the past, I had reservations about visiting this holy place, because it was associated with the Catholic faith and I wasn't sure if I would feel comfortable there. However, on this day, when Linda suggested that we stop and visit, I agreed.

We wandered up a paved path with high mountain laurels on either side of us. Tucked into them were bronze and stone monuments depicting the Stations of the Cross. Rosary prayer was unfamiliar to me and Linda quietly explained this and other Catholic customs as we reverently walked the path to the grotto. We soon came into an open area, and saw a small, quaint, stone chapel where Elizabeth Seton, who founded the first American Catholic School, used to pray.

As we continued around the chapel, I saw the grotto; a shallow cave nestled in the hillside. The story of St. Bernadette and the apparitions of Mary she witnessed in Lourdes, France in 1858 were unknown to me. Linda pointed out the statuary and explained the story as we respectfully approached the grotto. The ceiling to the cave was several feet taller than us at the entrance and sloped downward towards the back. I was mindful of ducking my head as I took several steps inside. The walls were black from years of candle smoke, and we breathed in the scent of warm wax. Stepping within the U-shaped tiered candle stand, I felt the glow of lit candles on my face and experienced a sense of peace and calm as I watched the dancing flames.

Following Linda's lead, I wrote a prayer on a piece of paper and slipped it into the receptacle. We both prayed silently as we took the flame from a burning candle and lit new ones. The place and the practice were unfamiliar to me, yet I found it strangely compelling. As I left the cave, I noticed a short waterfall nearby and wandered over to it. I listened to the bubbling water and watched it travel under the rustic stone shrine; noticing the unexpected blend of nature and religion in these mountain woods. I continued to walk slowly through these sacred grounds, taking in every detail. I felt a strange mixture of connection and other-worldliness at the same time. Old and new worlds came together in a unique and special way in this place, as ancient legends of faith met and provided a safe harbor for present-day stories.

As I walked, I noticed that my breathing was being transformed. It became deeper and slower and had a tangible quality to it that was unlike anything I had experienced before. I felt an energy that could only be described as holy. Throughout the grounds old boxwood bushes loomed large and towered over our heads. As Linda and I walked, they gave off a strong scent. Feeling something strange coming over me, I sat down on a bench and focused on the chapel in front of me. I gazed up at the sky and trees above and unexpectedly saw in their shapes the face of Jesus. I sat there transfixed; absorbing the vision and savoring this holy and special place.

I gradually noticed a large boxwood bush nearby. It was tall and hollowed out in the center, creating a cave-like entrance to an inner world beneath its green leaves. Something was bothering me about it. The scent of the boxwoods was triggering a memory. I shut my eyes and saw my little girl hiding in the hollowed out bush. She was very small, dirty, and frightened. In my vision, I coaxed her out and she came and sat on the bench with me. Her blonde hair was long and matted, and it framed her dirt-stained face. She wouldn't look at me, but instead averted her eyes and cast them down and away from human contact. This dimension of my inner child had been hiding for many years and now squinted in the bright light. I became aware of Jesus and his mother Mary, who were now sitting on either side of my little girl. They spoke comforting words to her, and reassured her that it was safe to come out now. Mary wiped the hair away from the little girl's eyes and gently stroked her forehead. Mary said that it was okay to trust Jesus to take care of her, and the little girl turned towards him and climbed up on his lap and laid her head against his shoulder. I could sense that she could feel the rough texture of his robe and the warmth of his presence and found comfort there. During this vision, my eyes were closed and I noticed that my breathing was deep, rhythmic, and somewhat labored as it filled my lungs.

Linda had joined me on the bench while I was in this meditative state and was silently praying. She was present but did not interrupt what was happening. My little girl took hold of Jesus' and Mary's hands, and knew that she could leave this place and take them with her. I opened my eyes and returned to the vision of Jesus' face in the sky and trees, and knew something profound had just occurred. The healing was swift and silent, yet powerful and transformative. God moved to heal my heart when I was ready to receive this healing.

The lost child inside of me was venturing out and starting to trust that it was safe to be in the world again. By placing my child's confidence in Jesus and Mary, I purposefully chose to align myself with a source of security and strength that could never be taken away. In the days and weeks following those experiences at the workshop and the Grotto, my adult confidence grew stronger as the child in me was healed. I found myself stepping more fully into my work and showing up in the world in a new way. Experiences of my past helped me to empathize with others, which was instrumental in my work as a coach.

Although I have always had a playful side, I found a distinct difference in my ability to experience joy as my inner child continued to heal. A little over a year after my healing experience at the Grotto, this playful side blossomed in me when I had the opportunity to travel to Germany and

> The healing was swift and silent, yet powerful and transformative.

Switzerland. This trip granted me 10 days of enchanting moments, which graced my life at a time when I was surprisingly receptive. Typically, I find that traveling ignites my sense of adventure as I step out of my comfort zone to meet new people and engage in fresh experiences. Relieved of my normal routine, I am usually more open and relaxed when on the road. Occasionally, it can also evoke some anxiety as I expand the boundaries of my knowledge, perspectives, and relationships.

In this instance, I was able to trust my partially healed heart as I relaxed my sense of responsibility to let the child within me come out and play more fully. It was during this trip that the third healing of my heart unexpectedly occurred when God moved silently yet powerfully at a place called Wieskirch or The Church in the Meadow. It was there that I experienced more profound changes in my heart and soul.

The path to this third healing actually began well before the trip occurred when God guided not only my decision to travel, but also who my traveling companions would be on this incredible journey.

CHAPTER SEVEN
REFLECTION QUESTIONS

Discovering Your Heart Healings

1. What has been your experience with different faith communities? What have you learned from those encounters?

2. In what ways has your heart been healed?

3. Many people have suffered some form of abuse or another. What do you make of the statement: 'a person doesn't need to remember the details of abuse for healing to occur'?

4. Wounded and broken hearts are a universal experience. What techniques or practices have you used to heal the wounds of your heart?

5. What are the sources of your security and strength?

PART 2
A Distinct Difference:
Revelations in Germany

Invitation to a Journey

"Have you ever heard of Oberammergau?" I asked my friend Linda as we walked the streets of our neighborhood. Linda and I initially met through our youngest children and became walking buddies when they went off to college. As we each adjusted to the empty nest phase of our lives, we had more free time to grow a friendship based on mutual interests. In her early fifties, Linda brought an appealing balance of playfulness and spirituality to our friendship. She has a sense of humor that frequently leads her to laugh loud and hard, often at herself; and I like that about her. Linda was raised Catholic which was a denomination where I had historically felt unwelcome. But our common interest in spirituality led to many open and deep discussions in which we pondered the mystery of God and further developed our ever evolving faiths. It was a special joy to have such a fun-loving yet reflective friend. We enjoyed observing and discussing God's presence in our daily lives and the ongoing challenges of trusting His Divine presence and guidance.

"No what is it?" she replied.

"It's this amazing place in Germany where every 10 years the villagers perform the Passion of Christ play," I said. "They've carried on this tradition since the time of the Black Plague; so for 375 years they've put on this production to honor God. It began when the villagers prayed to God to spare them from the plague as it swept across Europe killing thousands. They promised God that if He spared their village, they would honor Him every decade by performing the Passion Play. Christians throughout the years have traveled from all over the world to see this rendition of Christ's last days."

I went on to explain that my mother had long desired to travel with me. Whenever she had suggested it though, I always had a reason not to go. As a single mom, I felt that I could not afford the expense or the time away from my sons and our family activities. While this was true, to be honest, there was also a part of me that thought it might be stressful to travel with my mom. I loved her dearly, but I was not sure I wanted to be her travel partner. I had visions of being on a senior citizen tour bus with a bunch of doddering old people who walked with canes and went to sleep at 9:00 PM each night.

To be fair, though, my mother is an energetic and active senior, and she is not at all doddering. In fact, I'm envious of all the places she has traveled to in her lifetime. She makes travel a priority and plans wonderful trips, usually accompanied by a friend. There was another part of me that regretted that I had always found a reason not to travel with Mom.

Despite all of these previous hesitations, however, when she showed me the brochure for a tour to Oberammergau with her church, I immediately knew that this was our trip to do together. I had never heard about the village or the play, but was instantly aware that this was something I wanted to do and needed to see. More and more, I was learning that God has a gentle way of guiding me to know what I need to do without a lot of fanfare or attention. I was trusting my inner wisdom which said, *This is it,* and in doing so, I committed to going on the trip with Mom.

Something else nudged me, however, to suggest that we each invite a traveling buddy. We agreed that Mom would invite her friend Bobby and that I would also ask someone to travel with me. In this way we would each have a companion our own age. If I was going on this adventure, I wanted to be able to enjoy the night life and stay up later than Mom's bedtime!

After prayerful consideration and research, Bobby and Linda both accepted our invitations to take this trip with us. Bobby and Mom had traveled successfully together in the past. Being new friends, Linda and I weren't sure what it would be like to travel together. I was confident, however, that we could work through any issues which might come up. We were excited and a little nervous because we had no idea what God had in store for us. But, we had each said "yes" to the trip and "yes" to God working in our lives through this incredible opportunity.

CHAPTER EIGHT
REFLECTION QUESTIONS

Discovering Your
Spiritual Journey

1. With whom in your life do you have conversations about faith?

2. How do you recognize your inner wisdom ?

3. What journeys have helped you to expand your faith?

4. What emotions did you experience when taking those journeys?

Companions on a Journey

We landed in Frankfurt, Germany at 6:00 AM after traveling all night. I was tired, wrinkled, bleary-eyed, and excited. As we stood around the baggage claim area waiting for our luggage to arrive, I took stock of the cast of characters that God had brought together for this pilgrimage to Oberammergau. Our tour group was comprised of 35 adventurous travelers, and a subset within that group was our little troupe of companions. There was, of course, Linda, my travel buddy. This was her first time traveling to Europe and the experience of flying all night was new to her. I noticed that she had a tired look of expectation on her face. In fact, we were all wearing that expression.

The central person in our subgroup was my mother, Nancy, who knew more people on the trip than the rest of us. A spry 79-year-old woman with an inquisitive mind, Mom is an avid learner and has been a lifelong traveler. She loves meeting new people, and she will unabashedly start a conversation with just about anyone to learn their life story. Her friendliness disarms people, and they freely tell her about themselves. Like many daughters, I have not always appreciated my mother's quirky qualities. I now recognize similar traits in myself, however, and embrace the similarities between Mom and me more and more. Mom had waited 10 years to do a trip with me and I could tell that her level of excitement was high.

Mom's friend, Bobby, had traveled with her over the years to many wonderful places (the Galapagos Islands being one of the more exotic trips). They shared a love of adventure that was contagious and irresistible. Despite the fact that Bobby had traveled extensively with my mom in the past, I had only met her for the first time when we prepared for this trip. My initial impression was that she was just like my mom, and that I liked her. Bobby was a slightly built woman in her early seventies with short-cropped curly hair. She and my mom looked so much alike they could have been sisters. Since my mom doesn't have any siblings, I was delighted that she had found a sister-of-the-heart. Bobby moved quickly and took in everything with her bright blue eyes. She didn't miss much, and I could see the close friendship that she and

Mom enjoyed. I was glad she was on the trip with us, and I felt reassured that between the two of us we would take good care of my mom.

The fifth member of our troupe was Annemarie; a short, gray-haired woman who was my mother's neighbor and friend. She was a spirited octogenarian with a great sense-of-humor and a love for telling stories. Annemarie was born in Germany and she still had a strong accent, despite living in the U.S. for many years. She had a custom of traveling back to Germany every other year to visit family and friends. Annemarie had never seen the Passion Play at Oberammergau, however, and she chose to join my mom's church tour to her homeland on this particular year. She decided to travel as a single in order to have a room to herself each night.

Annemarie had an oversized beige leather purse that she hugged to her chest since it held everything that they specifically tell you not to carry as a tourist; all of her cash, her passport, and her credit cards. Due to a bad knee, she walked a little slowly, but never expected anyone to make special accommodations for her. I had met Annemarie previously at a few social functions with my mom, but didn't know her well. She was easy to like and I felt an instant connection between us. The twinkle in her eye and her droll sense of humor had endeared her to me before the trip even began.

I looked around at these three gray-haired women and Linda, and I could feel the electric excitement that emanated from all of our faces. We were finally here in Germany after a long nighttime flight over the Atlantic.

Our spiritual leader for this adventure was Kim, a 38-year-old African-American woman who was also traveling as a single on the trip. She had a broad smile that radiated incredible enthusiasm. We would soon learn that she would begin every morning on our tour bus with a booming loud voice, "Good morning, my good people," and then share some Scripture and her gold nugget for the day. We would also soon discover that she had unbridled enthusiasm for all aspects of the journey; which not only included the flock she was shepherding, but also good food (especially fine chocolates). She was another woman who loved adventure and travel.

This trip was supposed to have been Kim's vacation from the demands of shepherding her own church community as its pastor. When the original minister who planned and organized our tour discovered that he couldn't go, he asked Kim if she would lead the pilgrimage in his place. With some hesitation she had accepted. She agreed to be the spiritual leader and planned to leave the day-to-day details to the tour guide and bus driver. God put her in the right place at the right time; her leadership was a blessing to all of us, and the trip in turn would become a blessing to her own growth.

We soon saw our tour guide, Jeff, standing by the baggage claim, holding a sign to identify our tour group. Since I had never traveled with a tour guide before I was curious what he would be like.

Jeff was a bit on the shorter side of average height. He was wearing a white, casual, button-down shirt with gold-rimmed reading glasses stuck in the pocket, and khaki-colored cargo pants with big side pockets that had something in them that rattled when he walked. He later showed us it was a tin of mints, which I noticed he popped in his mouth when he was trying to maintain his patience with certain members of the tour group (since he wasn't allowed to smoke while on duty). He also wore Crocs on his feet and a white bucket hat, like Gilligan wore in the 1960's sitcom. A day pack was slung over his shoulders from which he would occasionally pull out a red windbreaker when it rained or an old gray sweater when it got chilly. Other than that, this was pretty much his uniform for most of the trip.

Jeff looked fit and a little rough around the edges in an intriguing sort of way. He had soft brown eyes with curly lashes, a constant five o'clock shadow, and a beaming smile when he chose to share it. But it was Jeff's voice that really struck me the most about him. He had an English accent, which he often used with a lot of inflection; aptly conveying his dry sense-of-humor.

Our bus driver, Werner, was waiting for us outside of the terminal. He was a soft-spoken man with a thick German accent and his hair pulled back in a ponytail. In the same way that Jeff's accent caught my attention and delighted me, what I noticed most about Werner were his incredibly well defined muscles; the largest I had ever seen in person on a man. I couldn't help but admire them while he drove us all over Germany and Switzerland. He skillfully navigated us through the narrow and busy streets of Frankfurt and Heidelberg, the cobblestone alleys of Boppard and Rothenberg, and the windy roads on the way to Zurich. Werner could maneuver our bus into any parking space at a tourist attraction with ease. With his eyes and attention always on the road ahead of us, he truly was our driving angel. God, however, was our ultimate navigator on this journey; always present, guiding, and providing everything that we needed…as well as some surprises.

As we left the airport, Werner drove our tour bus through Frankfurt to visit the first of many cathedrals that we would see on our trip. Once inside, each of us wandered off on our own to absorb the enormity of this edifice to God. The gold and gilded statuaries arranged in the various alcoves drew me forward, and I paused in front of several of them to appreciate the artist's renditions of scenes from the Bible. I noticed that a few people seated in the pews were praying, and I felt a twinge of guilt at interrupting their spiritual time with our picture snapping and exclamations of *oohs* and *aahs*. It felt almost sacrilegious to be touring a place of worship while people were actively engaged in prayer.

After wandering around for a bit, several of us settled into pews to simply sit and be still. Pastor Kim was seated a few rows ahead of me, and she was telling those around her how cathedrals are constructed to carry sound. There were no acoustical aides long ago, she explained, so the building itself was the aid. Knowing that she was a singer, someone asked her to sing a note so that we could hear how it carried in the cathedral. She obliged and sang the first line of the Our Father prayer. She was right, the sound carried beautifully throughout the magnificent building. Kim continued to sing the prayer slowly and gracefully, interlacing the notes through the air like a master weaver. Everyone in the church became still as we received the music she offered as a gift to God, and to us. We were motionless and silent as she finished the prayer song, in awe of her vocal talent and the acoustics of this ancient stately cathedral.

A single traveler in our group named Joanne was also a singer. She pointed to grates in the floor where soloists would have stood on a lower level, and explained how their voice would have carried, just as Kim's had, when singing for the congregants. I was inspired by the visual and auditory beauty around me, and savored the graceful words and sentiments with which Kim had blessed us.

Kim's prayer song was still lingering in my soul later that day as we sat at an outdoor balcony overlooking the Rock of Lorelei on a legendary bend of the Rhine River. I was enjoying the company, food, and beautiful scenery while listening attentively as Annemarie told stories about growing up in Germany. She was describing how her father traveled the countryside drilling wells for water. Throughout the trip, she would tell us many stories that gave us an account of what growing up in this country was like from a young girl's perspective. Her personal viewpoints provided a balance to the tour guides' explanations, enriching our understanding of Germany's intense history.

After Annemarie finished this particular story, I gazed over the Rhine and was struck by the color of the water; greenish in hue with no eddies or rocks, and a smooth consistent flow. The barge traffic was nonstop, and many of the boats had upper decks with bikes, toys, and floats. Annemarie explained that the captains often lived on the barges with their families and carried their life's belongings with them on the river. Time seemed to stand still as I lifted my face to the sun, feeling God's presence soak into me. I silently thanked Him for bringing me here with these special women.

I had worked so hard to heal my broken heart during the past 10 years and I gratefully embraced the lightheartedness of this long-awaited vacation. I knew God had led me here and I now eagerly anticipated what He would show me in the days ahead. Absorbing the beauty of this place on a warm afternoon, I could tell that with this incredible group of women, we were going to have a fabulous trip together. It was a moment to treasure as we raised our glasses and joined in a toast, "To Germany!" With the warmth of the sun on my skin, and the friendly faces surrounding me, I was aware of being deeply content and happy.

CHAPTER NINE
REFLECTION QUESTIONS
Discovering Travel Wisdom

1. What have been your experiences when traveling with others?

2. What were the challenges and blessings of these experiences?

3. What did you learn about yourself from them?

4. What do you think about the concept that traveling stretches you and may reveal new aspects of yourself, such as your inner child or perhaps anxiety?

5. In what ways do you feel the presence of God when you travel?

CHAPTER *10*

Oxbows

Some of us were better at acclimating to group travel than others. Annemarie, Linda, and I were accustomed to independent travel, so being part of a tour group was unfamiliar and challenging at times. This also resulted in a few situations that were not only amusing, but were opportunities for God's grace to be revealed. The first of these occurred in the quaint town of Boppard when Linda and I opted to take our own tour of the town instead of joining Jeff's guided walk.

One of the most striking things we noticed in Germany was the presence of profusely overflowing flower baskets everywhere. Germans clearly took pride in their green thumbs and did not hold back when it came to floral displays. As we wandered along the water's edge in Boppard, we were torn between gazing at the winding Rhine River with the low lying hills beyond it, and beholding the quaint painted houses and abundant flower displays in the town itself. Linda snapped pictures as we walked and enjoyed the beauty of this village on the river. Arriving at the end of our path, we decided to wander up a hill into town. We noticed signs pointing to a chair lift, and out of curiosity, we followed them.

In addition to being independent, Linda and I can both be a bit impulsive at times, and have a tendency for doing things on the spur of the moment...one of those moments was about to occur. We approached the chair lift and gazed up the hills towards the top, wondering where it would take us. We each had the necessary Euros in our pockets for the fare, and asked the ticket vendor how long it would take to go up and back. We discussed whether we had enough time to ride the lift and still make it back to the hotel in time for dinner.

Following the line of the cables with my eyes to the top of the hill, I succumbed to the lure of the unknown. The promise of an adventure on our own beckoned us forward. We bought our tickets, and stood in place to be scooped up by the chair as it swept around the pillar at the base of the lift. We chatted excitedly as the chair caught us and we glided up and over the hills, affording us a panoramic view of the surrounding area. We could see further and further over the landscape as we ascended, and I was glad we decided to do this. I smiled as I enjoyed the thrill of venturing out on our own free of the larger group and our tour guide.

As we approached the top, we were a bit confused as to where we should hop off the lift and we subsequently overshot the exit spot. As we did so, two men in attendance of the lift started talking to us in an animated way, clearly urging us to do something. Since they spoke in German, we had no idea what they were saying. We responded in English, egotistically hoping they would switch to our language, but they did not. As the chair rounded the top and started to go back down the slope, one man urgently gestured for to us to jump off, which we did, although none too gracefully. As we stumbled away from the chair, we laughed at ourselves and the funny look on the lift man's face when he had urged us to jump off. He took his cigarette out of his mouth and started guffawing and hacking at the same time, unable to control the coughing fit that came with his unexpected laughter.

We shook our heads as we walked away, laughing and apologizing for missing our cue to exit at the right time. It was exhilarating being on top of this hill; laughing, walking, talking, and soaking up the carefree independence of being off on our own. We were surprised to see that there were several paths and, after checking our watches, decided we had time to walk down one of them to explore. Our sense of adventure grew as we came out of the woods into a large open area with a low-lying building. Beyond it we saw a wide stone patio shaded by a canopy of huge trees with tables for outdoor dining. It was inviting and beckoned us to take a closer look. We saw diners leisurely enjoying late afternoon refreshments at several of the tables and courteously skirted around them to the edge of the patio. We caught our breath as we took in the view before us.

The Rhine River we had been following all day curved into an oxbow in the scene below us. In a slow, undulating fashion it turned completely in the opposite direction. From where we stood it looked like a giant letter "U" carved into the landscape. I marveled at this surprising view and again was thankful that we had taken the opportunity to venture out on our own. It felt as if God had led us to this restful place with a clear vantage of the river's course.

Linda and I couldn't resist the temptation to sit at the edge of this spectacular view and bask in it for a while. As we placed our drink order, we reflected together how life can be like a river; you never know what is around the next bend. There are times when we can rise above the day-to-day course of events and glimpse a clearer view. This oxbow reminded us that sometimes life makes a complete U- turn. While in the midst of the daily actions that lead to change, we don't always see the larger picture. I silently thanked God for leading us to this special place and for providing this visual reminder that He was directing the flow of events in my life just like He directed the course of this river.

When our drinks arrived, our conversation turned to discussing a mutual friend who had recently told us she was falling in love with a man she had been dating for some time. Linda shared that she missed our friend, who had been spending a great deal of time with her new beau. I noted that the changes to our friendship had a different impact on me. Instead of feeling the loss, I struggled with envy. I tried not to think

> This oxbow reminded us that sometimes life makes a complete U-turn.

about it too much because it made me acutely aware that I didn't have a loving relationship with a man. I was happy for our friend, yet jealous of her joy at the same time.

At this point in my life I had been divorced for seven years, and although I dated during this time period, I had never fallen in love with anyone. Most of my dating relationships were enjoyable but never went very deep. I felt a companionable love for a longtime friend that I dated on and off over the years, but it wasn't the disorienting falling-in-love feeling that our mutual friend was experiencing.

I commented to Linda, "I'm not sure I can even fall in love anymore. At 51 I doubt it can happen to me. I'm happy that she has found someone special. It's hard to be around her sometimes though, because it reminds me of what I don't have." Again our gaze returned to the oxbow river below us as we contemplated the twists and turns of relationships. A gift had been given to us in this elevated view of the river and we lingered, pondering it for a bit longer from this shaded vantage point before returning to the hotel.

Despite our best efforts, our little excursion caused us to be late for dinner and we rushed to join the others in the dining room. Our traveling companions were somewhat concerned regarding our whereabouts, but then became curious to hear about our independent adventure. Jeff seemed relieved to have us present and accounted for, and smiled with a thoughtful expression as we enthusiastically described the chair lift and the view of the oxbow in the river to everyone.

As we ate, I talked with Pastor Kim and learned more about this interesting young woman. She told me her story about becoming a pastor and some of the challenges she had to overcome in order to do so. I found myself taking quite a liking to her. She was open, honest, and passionate about her faith. I admired her connection to God and everyone with whom she interacted. I sensed at that moment that she had been chosen for this trip, and that God was working through her.

We listened to two of our fellow travelers, Sue and Jack, as they talked about other trips they had taken together. Someone from our group assumed that they were married and Sue quickly corrected her. "Oh, we're not married," she said, with a sheepish glance at Pastor Kim. She went on in a somewhat justifying tone, "It's not Jack's fault. He's a great guy. I just don't trust marriage after my last one, so I am the one holding things up." Jack looked on and smiled at her while she self-consciously explained their relationship to the rest of us seated around the table.

I could certainly relate to Sue; divorce has a way of leaving one afraid to fall in love and commit to a relationship again. A skeptical view of love can emerge as we try to protect ourselves from more heartache. I watched Jack and Sue together, clearly seeing how much they treasured one another, and felt a connection with this woman who vulnerably shared her fears with us. My heart warmed with empathy for her and I felt a twinge of encouragement that perhaps it was possible to find love in mid-life.

While I wasn't actively searching for romance, thoughts of it surfaced more frequently as I observed some of my peers venturing into this realm. After my earlier discussion with Linda, I wondered if my envy was slowly transforming into a nugget of hope as I witnessed others navigating this territory of the heart successfully. Still feeling skeptical about the notion of romantic love, I noticed that recently it was becoming easier for me to love more freely in my non-romantic relationships such as in my newfound friendship with Annemarie.

CHAPTER TEN
REFLECTION QUESTIONS

Discovering Your Oxbows

1. 'Life can be like a river; you never know what is around the next bend.' What does this statement mean to you?

2. In what ways has your life taken a U-turn? What did you learn from that experience?

3. In what ways have you ventured out on your own?

4. What were the surprises and/or rewards from making that move?

5. What triggers envy or loneliness in you?

6. The painful loss of a significant loving relationship can leave us afraid to trust love again. What comes up for you when you consider this statement?

Annemarie

Annemarie, being a native of Germany, was a great resource especially when we dined together on our trip. At our first meal, she ordered Wiener Schnitzel and a Radler, which was a drink consisting of beer, Sprite, and a squeeze of lemon. Linda and I wrinkled our noses with distaste at the idea of mixing beer and soda and ordered a local Pilsner instead. When the Radler arrived, Annemarie said, "Taste it!" in her thick German accent as her brown eyes twinkled with delight.

Being a home-brewer, Linda was interested in tasting as many different types of German beers as possible on this trip, but I could see that she truly did not want to sample this one. Trying to avoid hurting Annemarie's feelings Linda raised the glass of Radler to her mouth and pretended to drink it, but instead just wet her lips. Annemarie wasn't fooled and called her on it, saying, "No, take a *real* drink." With a sheepish look, Linda obeyed.

"Okay, that's enough," Annemarie said, abruptly grabbing her glass back. This would be their dining dialog throughout the trip as Annemarie would encourage Linda to try new food and drinks, and then limit how much she could have. Her offers to taste were always, "Try some, but not too much!"

Annemarie's sincere yet mischievous encouragement for Linda to take real samples of food and beer was equally matched whenever she playfully tried to instruct me to speak German. I was bound and determined to correctly pronounce the foreign words I was learning, and Annemarie was more than happy to help. She would face me, purse her lips together, and make a phlegmy sound in her throat as she repeated whatever word I was attempting to say. Usually I would get it wrong the first time and require further instruction. Sometimes she would even grab my cheeks with one hand and squeeze them together to pucker my lips like a fish, in an effort to get the right sound out of them.

I would try to imitate her rolling *r*'s and guttural throat sounds over and over again until I got her nod of approval. "Ja, that's goot, Ca*rrrr*ol," she would say, and I would relax with a satisfied smile. Despite the difficulty of learning the language I found myself relishing the gentle teasing this German grandmother lovingly bestowed upon me. Annemarie's light-hearted, teasing nature was counter-balanced by her independent and headstrong qualities… as we would soon find out.

En route to the dock for a four-hour boat ride on the Rhine River, Jeff's droll voice came over the bus speakers, explaining important details about our connection with the river boat. He clearly and patiently provided us with the details we would need to know to make a smooth connection. I didn't mind the hand-holding; telling us where to go, what to do, and when to do it. It was helpful and I unexpectedly found myself grateful for his guidance. I thought having a tour guide would be tedious and restrictive, but in fact, I found just the opposite to be true. It was nice not having to think about the details, and I found myself relaxing and genuinely enjoying the experience. This was a strange sensation for me, since I always liked to be independent. I was surprised at my newfound sense of inter-dependence and connection with this group.

As we gathered at the dock to wait for the river boat, members of our group stood in small clusters, talking and getting better acquainted with one another. After a few minutes had passed, my mother approached me with a worried expression, prompting me to ask what was wrong. She said, "It's Annemarie. She told me that she wanted to get her phone activated and that she was going across the street into that store to have it done. She should have been back by now." Mom stood and looked across the street at the store as she said this, as if by doing so it would compel Annemarie to appear.

Jeff approached us and said, "The boat will be here any minute and Annemarie is missing." You could clearly see the displeasure and concern on his face.

Jeff asked Mom where Annemarie had said she was going and we all became concerned as the gravity of the situation dawned on us. Jeff told those of us who had gathered around that we should board the boat when it arrived. He pointed and said, "I'm going to head up the street and take a look for her there in those shops." I watched Jeff as he hurried off and observed that he was focused on one thing only; reclaiming one of his lost sheep and bringing her back to the fold. We watched from the dock to see if he would be successful, silently praying for Annemarie's safe return. It seemed like such a small town that I was sure he would find her. After all, she was a slow-moving, eighty-year-old woman with a bad knee, so how far could she have wandered?

Jeff returned within 10 minutes, anxiously asking us if she had returned on her own. I replied, "No," as the horn of the large river boat loudly announced its arrival at the dock. Jeff hurried to tell the pier captain that we were missing one of our members, as the rest of us gathered together by the gangplank and prepared to board the boat. The drama continued to unfold as Jeff told the captain that he wanted to send the rest of us on without him while he waited by the dock. The pier captain insisted that Jeff stay with his tour group, and assured him that she would send Annemarie to the next port by way of a taxi whenever she showed up.

Jeff was the last one of us to board the boat and he only did so because the pier captain practically shoved him on board. He was clearly distressed at having lost one of his charges, and rightly so. It was only the second day of the trip and already we were missing one of our members. As the boat left the pier, I said a silent prayer for Annemarie's quick and safe return to our group and then turned to climb the stairs to the broad upper deck. I felt a warm breeze on my face as I observed people sitting and enjoying refreshments while the boat chugged steadily up the river. There were commuters as well as tourists on board, and once again I found myself appreciating the slower pace of this country. Even the non-tourists seemed relaxed and appeared to be thoroughly enjoying a leisurely cruise on this summer day.

A half hour into our boat ride I ran into Jeff, who was anxiously pacing back and forth. His phone rang while we were talking. It was the pier captain, calling to tell him that Annemarie had arrived at the dock and was being put in a taxi, which would drive her to the next port-of-call. She would be able to board the boat there. Greatly relieved, Jeff thanked the pier captain and hung up with a grin. His confidence returned as he announced to everyone that Annemarie would be joining us at the next stop. There was a collective sigh of relief from our entire tour group. I said a silent thank you to God. Assured that our lost sheep would soon be returning to the fold, we all finally relaxed and began enjoying our riverboat ride up the Rhine.

Mom, Bobby, Linda, and I gathered four chairs together and settled ourselves to watch the passing view. As the river boat paddles churned through the water, the sun warmed the boat's painted green decking. The warmth radiated upwards onto us and the surrounding lounging passengers. Small castles were strategically situated high above the river overlooking their domain. The steep hillsides on either side of the river had rows upon rows of grapevines neatly trellised; traversing in various directions like a patchwork quilt. Occasionally, we would point out a worker in the vineyards and exclaim how small he looked on the steep hillsides. The look and feel of this area was other-worldly, as if I'd gone back in time.

The river boat captain's voice came over the loudspeaker telling us the names of every castle and town that we passed. It wasn't long before he announced that we were approaching the next port of call, and we all gathered around the railing to look for Annemarie. Jeff headed down the stairs to greet her while the rest of us waited above deck. Soon she appeared and we hooted and hollered and waved to her as she walked down the gangplank and boarded the boat. She was clearly embarrassed by all the fuss, but that didn't stop some of the group from taking pictures to document her return.

The entire tour group was clearly relieved and happy to have Annemarie back.

After speaking with Jeff, she was greeted with a great cheer as she joined our group. She was an instant celebrity. She was surrounded by relieved tour members who expressed their heartfelt greetings. I made my way over to her and gave her a hug saying, "I'm so glad you are back safe and sound. You had us worried!" I happened to catch Jeff's eye as I lavished my attention on dear, sweet, funny Annemarie. I could see his quiet pleasure at the reuniting of our little pod of travelers.

We found a chair for Annemarie to sit in as she joined our circle. Someone said, "Annemarie, what did it feel like when you got back to the dock and realized we had left without you?" She made a surprised and anxious face and several cameras snapped her expression as the rest of us laughed. Worry was replaced by delight now that we had our Annemarie back with us, and all was right with the world again.

As everyone returned to their seats and left us alone, Annemarie said in her strong German accent, "Oh Carrrol, I shouldn't have left the group. I thought I could find the shop the first storeowner sent me to, so that I could get my phone done before the boat came. I thought it was coming at ten-thirty, not ten o'clock." The twinkle had left her eyes and it was replaced by a worried expression and a discouraged tone. "I'm too old to be doing this trip. I don't know why I came."

Her eyes pleaded for reassurance and I gave it to her without hesitation. "Nonsense, Annemarie, you were meant to be on this trip. We will look after you. We will look after one another," I said as I patted her arm. Her shoulders relaxed and she said, "Thank you. I am so glad I am traveling with you and your mother."

"Besides," I added, "what would we do without you to tell us how to order our Wiener Schnitzel and beer?" Her shoulders shook as she gently laughed and I reached out to hug her close. I thought that this was such a dear soul that God had brought into my life. Her grandmotherly charm and wisdom, enhanced by her strong accent and proclivity for mischief, endeared her to my heart more and more each day. We seemed to need each other. I reflected that despite the difference in years, the joyful child inside both Annemarie and me seemed to come out to play when we were together. I thought about how the years slip away and how age doesn't matter when your heart recognizes a playmate.

I settled into a luxuriously lazy frame of mind, which felt wholly delicious after the anxiety of the past few hours. Linda and I decided to take a leisurely stroll and climbed the steps at the rear of the boat, where we leaned against the railing and watch the churning water left in the boat's wake. We chatted about the incredible views and laughed about Annemarie's adventure. With the wind in my hair and the sun on my face, I shut my eyes and soaked in this moment. I recognized again that I was deeply content to be here. I felt peaceful down to my soul and incredibly lighthearted at the same time.

This contrast of feelings was new for me. I am typically a very active woman who can, at times, allow busyness to obscure what is most important in life. I found myself settling into a rhythm on this trip that allowed me to let go of my daily concerns and just *be* in the moment. This was something I had often talked about and longed for, yet found the reality of it hard to achieve. I was surprised to find myself experiencing it on this trip in an effortlessly refreshing way.

Linda and I saw the Rudesheim port in the distance and soon descended the stairs to rejoin Mom, Bobby, and Annemarie. They were standing on the deck listening to Jeff as he answered questions and gave directions to our group. I approached my mother and gave her a spontaneous hug and kiss on the cheek. My mom and I are usually not physically demonstrative, but something was different about our relationship on this trip. I felt a more loving connection with her, and deeply appreciated being on this journey together. It was as if the child in each of us had also come out to play. She wasn't just my mother here but my friend, too; a friend that I loved dearly and appreciated as I witnessed her sharing her passion for adventure and travel with us all.

Jeff smiled at our brief exchange, and we refocused our attention on what he was saying. I noticed that our little travel troupe felt even closer since we recovered Annemarie. We were becoming a tight-knit group and I liked that feeling.

These were my people and I felt loved and accepted among these older, wiser women.

As the boat approached the dock we prepared to disembark and venture into the town of Rudesheim. Everyone jokingly asked if Annemarie was with us and she took the kidding in stride. I have to admit that I was keeping more of a watchful eye on her, as were others in the group; a theme that would continue throughout the rest of our trip together.

Now with my arm locked in Annemarie's, we focused our attention on Jeff to hear about the next stage of our adventure. Being nervous about losing someone, Jeff was, once again, trying to count all of us to make sure everyone was present. Actually, we were all a bit nervous about losing another member of the group. Someone suggested that we assign ourselves individual numbers and then count off as an easy way for Jeff to account for everyone's presence. We readily agreed and proceeded to count off, military style. Kim, our pastor, was last and shouted out "Thirty-five, anchor!" to signify that the count was completed. We were all pleasantly amused at her sense-of-humor and recognized she was indeed anchoring us to God on this journey.

Satisfied that we now had a good method of accountability for everyone, we fell in step behind Jeff as he led us away from the river, across the street, and up a narrow alley full of shops and people. Touristy though it was, the alley felt cool as the tall buildings on either side of it created shade from the afternoon sun. It was crowded and our group strung along as some slowed to window shop and gaze about. We kept moving though, and ended up at a restaurant that Jeff had chosen for lunch. The inside of the building was dark and cool, and we stood there for a moment waiting for our eyes to adjust. There was an open sky courtyard at the center of the restaurant, and we gravitated towards its outdoor charm.

Annemarie, however, wanted to eat indoors where it was cooler, and proceeded to seat herself at a table near the wall. The courtyard was sunny and inviting, and people were already enjoying the lovely setting. There was a large tree in the center of the dining area, casting shade over a massive wooden table. Many of us moved towards it and seated ourselves. I decided to sit with a different group to get to know others on the tour and took a seat by Pastor Kim.

I noticed that Linda and my mother went back indoors to sit with Annemarie. Trusting that they were taking care of her, Bobby and I stayed seated at the table under the tree with six others. As we looked at the menus and considered our options, Linda tapped me on the shoulder and said that Annemarie had lost her purse and thought it might still be on the boat. I immediately went to speak with her as Linda took off in a hurry; hoping the boat hadn't already left the dock.

Mom and I brought Annemarie into the courtyard with us. She was understandably very distraught. In her large handbag she carried all of her important papers and *all* of her money for the trip...*in cash*! We had talked with her at length about using alternate forms of purchasing power, but to no avail. She was set in her ways and had told us that she always carried cash. Now her face was pale and stricken as she realized that she no longer had her purse and all that it contained. We seated her beside a fountain to wait for Linda, who would hopefully return with the purse in tow.

In the meantime, Linda, who had fortunately worn shorts and running shoes that day, raced down the alley, retracing our steps back to the dock. She was relieved to see that the boat was still there, but by now a crowd of people were gathered by the ropes, waiting to board the gangplank. Linda hurried past them, excusing herself while stepping over the rope. The captain loudly admonished her in German for this intrusion, but she rushed forward, explaining in English that she had just gotten off the boat and had left something important behind. She asked permission to search the areas where we had been. The disgruntled captain finally nodded in agreement, none too happy with this brash and desperate American woman.

Linda searched in vain. There was no handbag to be found on the boat. Hot and dripping with sweat, she returned to the restaurant and told us that her efforts had been unsuccessful. Linda asked Annemarie when she last remembered seeing her purse, and she replied that she thought she had it with her when she entered the restaurant. Linda went back inside to the table where Annemarie had first decided to sit. There, behind the tablecloth, next to the wall, was the handbag. Despite having looked under the table when she realized it was missing, Annemarie hadn't moved the cloth sufficiently and the bag had been hidden from her view.

Linda returned to our group, carrying the purse, and was greeted with loud applause. I looked at her face (and the rather crazed expression in her eyes), and then turned to Annemarie and said matter-of-factly, "You need to buy her a beer. Buy it *right now!*" I could see that my friend was hot, sweaty, and clearly annoyed at the stress and inconvenience of the past half hour as she ran all over town in search of a bag that was, in fact, in the restaurant the whole time.

As Linda sat down at the table, I pointed to the water spurting out of the mouth of the fish fountain beside her, and suggested that she stick her head in it to cool off. I have to be careful about what I say to Linda sometimes because she'll actually do it…and this was one of those times! Her wet head and face gave testimony to her impulsive decision to cool down right then and there. Chuckling and relieved, I returned to my seat at the other table and left Annemarie, Mom, and Linda to their conversation. I overheard Annemarie telling them how sorry she was and how an old woman like her shouldn't be traveling around like this. My mom and Linda were reassuring her, and I could see the relief in Annemarie's face as she realized everyone was committed to helping her.

I reflected on the challenges that we each faced in traveling together in this foreign land. Although I was grateful for the sense of security Jeff and Werner provided, I was also aware that it was important for us each to look out for one another. While it may feel exciting and adventuresome to go off on our own, it could also lead to problems, as some of us had already learned.

For me, there were lessons about independence and dependence woven among the magic moments of child-like wonder and joy on this trip. Being independent had led Annemarie astray, yet it had also led Linda and me to a place of beauty where we could see the oxbow curve of the river from high in the hills. Like the curve in the river, my life had taken a complete turn in another direction when I put my trust in God. I had purposefully chosen to go a new way when I climbed out of my pit of despair many years ago. The vantage view of the winding river seemed to be God's visual reminder to me of that fact.

Whether at home or on the road, I need God and fellow companions on the journey to help me stay on track and to avoid getting lost. I need God's guidance…and we all need one another. By first losing Annemarie herself, and then her handbag, we learned a lesson about the importance of staying connected and watching out for one another. This connected-ness holds true whether we were on a traveling adventure, or on the adventure of life itself.

CHAPTER ELEVEN
REFLECTION QUESTIONS
Discovering Interdependence

1. When have you become lost and figuratively 'missed the boat'? What did that feel like?

2. What experience have you had with determinedly heading out on your own?

3. Many of us grapple with being either overly dependent or independent. What helps you achieve interdependence with others?

4. What helps you to stay on-track and avoiding getting lost?

Tension, Tears, and Laughter

Our trip continued to offer lessons about the need for, and the challenges of, living in community, as well as opportunities for reconciliation. Traveling together in such close proximity highlighted mine and Linda's differences in our routines and expectations so that at times we were disappointed or irritated with one another. Tension grew between us until eventually we had a blow-up several days into the trip. The argument brought our issues out into the open where we could painfully, but honestly, address them. After our fears and tears were released, the strain dissipated and we were able to have a heartfelt conversation to restore harmony between us. The confrontation left each of us feeling tired and drained, but just as a thunderstorm can clear the humidity from the air, we felt refreshed by this honest communication.

Laura, a young woman in her thirties who was traveling with her mother on the trip, was also experiencing relationship stress and began to look more and more frazzled as the week went on. We ran into her at breakfast one day and invited her to eat with us. Laura sat down with a sigh and said "My mother is driving me crazy!" I raised my eyebrows at Linda as if to say, "See, other people have trouble getting along on vacation, too," and she knowingly smiled back at me. I asked Laura about it and she took a few moments to air her complaints about traveling with her mother. She went on to say, "Don't get me wrong. Mom brought me on this trip and I'm so grateful. It's just that she talks *ALL* the time and I need some quiet." I chuckled and told her how I am the same way and also needed silence at times.

Linda and I shared some of the difficulties we were experiencing and it felt good to know we weren't the only ones who were struggling in close quarters. I said, "Isn't it strange how we think vacations are going to be completely blissful experiences? We forget that people are still people even on vacation. We have happy moments and grumpy moments. We get out of sorts and need our space. I think it's perfectly normal for all of us to have relationship challenges here just like we do at home. In fact, even more so when we are on vacation because we are out of our routine and spend a lot of time in close proximity with others." We all agreed that there are certainly stresses involved with traveling. I could tell Laura felt better just for having talked about it. We agreed that it helps to know we are not alone in our feelings and that others are available to support us with a listening ear.

Our emotional stressors found a perfect release one evening when we dined at the famous Student Tavern in Heidelberg. The old paneled walls of the tavern were full of photos of past visitors, and the wooden doorways were covered with the carved initials of the students who had eaten there in the past. Our tour group was given one section of a back room. Mom, Bobby, Linda, Joanne, and I settled at a table on the outskirts of the group. The low ceilings and rustic wooden tables and benches gave it a cozy appeal, but with no carpeting on the floor the room was quite noisy. It was full of patrons and we raised our voices to be heard above the din. As we dug into our meals and tried to converse with one another, a slightly built Asian man with poker straight chin-length hair walked into the room and sat down at an upright piano that was situated right behind Linda and began to play.

Emotionally drained and frustrated by our inability to hear one another speak, we were trying to make the best of an already challenging situation. With the addition of music our annoyance bubble burst and we couldn't help but laugh at the absurdity of the piano player adding additional sound to the already noisy roomful of people. He was undaunted by our laughter and pounded out schmaltzy American tunes that his audience would recognize. I rolled my eyes at my tablemates and dramatically dropped my head into my hands. It was now impossible to have a conversation. I hoped that he would play just one song and then leave. But he went from one song right into another, and then another. Other patrons in the room clapped and I good-naturedly shouted, "Don't encourage him!" but to no avail.

He was fully in his groove now and was entertaining the noisy crowd with his repertoire of American tunes. Someone made a request and he turned to address the room. His salt and pepper hair hung straight and long about his ears, and his smile was broad and happy as he replied that he didn't know the song being requested. He explained that he didn't read music and slapped his palm against his forehead several times saying, "It's all in here." We held our sides laughing at his funny antics and gave into the preposterousness of this meal. It was not going to be a conversational evening. We could only make rolling eye contact with one another. Whenever one of us would try to talk, the rest of us would say "What?!" loudly, and then silently mouth the words "I can't hear you."

We were still fluctuating somewhere between annoyance and humor when he started to play the *Chicken Dance* song. At this point, Bobby succumbed to pure silliness. Seated beside my mom on a bench, she tucked her hands under her armpits and started flapping her slender arms like wings to the beat of the music. Her blue eyes took on a beady quality as she went through the dance motions with increasing intensity. We were soon in hysterics watching her movements become a blur of motion as the piano man played faster and faster. Her gyrations drew the attention of the other diners and soon the entire room was cheering her on. Reaching a feverish pitch she ended in a crescendo of arm flapping and hip wiggling in her seat and we all applauded her efforts. My sides hurt from laughing so much and I was grateful for this release after such a long and emotional day. It warmed my heart to know that Linda and I had bounced back from our low spot earlier in the day and were able to relax and enjoy ourselves again. I am convinced that a good belly laugh is one of the best ways to lift the heart and soul.

As we walked back to the hotel that night I reflected again how God seemed to be providing opportunities for us to be in relationship with Him, and each other, on this trip. Whether it was moments for connection and reconciliation, or moments of laughter and humor to lighten our hearts, we were being nurtured daily by His grace. We only need to look for these moments to see them. He was truly guiding and providing for all aspects of our care on this adventure. I reflected that no matter how much I think I am prepared for God's blessings, He frequently exceeds my expectations and blesses me more fully than I can imagine. I am humbled by His ever generous grace and provision. Walking in the glow of the setting sun in Heidelberg, I was overwhelmed with gratitude for the gifts of laughter and fellowship I had found with these fellow travelers.

CHAPTER TWELVE
REFLECTION QUESTIONS
Discovering Release

1. How do you release tension?

2. What do you know about 'relationship stress' that can occur while traveling?

3. What do you find are the benefits of a good belly laugh?

4. When have you experienced blessings that exceeded your expectations? What occurred?

CHAPTER 13

Communion on a Bus

Pastor Kim joined Linda, Bobby and I when we left the restaurant that night. We leisurely walked the cobblestoned streets while enjoying the view of the sun setting behind the Heidelberg castle, which almost seemed like a movie backdrop situated above the city. Kim proceeded to tell us she wanted to hold a small church service on the bus the following morning and offer Communion. She asked for our help in finding the necessary elements for the occasion. We were happy to assist her with this endeavor and brainstormed how we could do Communion on a bus. None of us had done this before and we rose to the challenge.

We stopped in several shops searching for grape juice and a loaf of bread. We found a bakery that was closing for the day and purchased the bread, however, we had no luck finding grape juice. Kim finally gave up and said we would have to use wine instead. We purchased a small bottle of red wine and two stout German wine goblets with sturdy green stems and wide, gold-rimmed bowls.

When Sunday dawned it was not only the day of our mobile church service, but it was also my birthday. Once we were under way, our bus became a traveling sanctuary. Pastor Kim began the service with her trademark broad smile and warm, booming voice as she greeted us with the now familiar, "Hello, good people!" She continued with, "Each day I have given you a golden nugget of God's wisdom as we travel to our next destination. It's been something for you to ponder and contemplate as you go through your day. Since today is the Lord's Day I want to share more with you and worship together to rejoice in appreciation for all that God is giving to us on this wonderful journey. Several members of our group have volunteered to help with this service. Joanne will lead us in song, Linda will read a Bible passage, and Carol will help me serve Communion. Having church on a moving bus is a first for me, so I hope it goes smoothly!"

She had my full attention and I anticipated how special it was going to feel to serve Communion on my birthday. We bowed our heads to pray with Pastor Kim and my heart warmed as she recognized and prayed specifically in celebration of my birthday, among other things. The glow I was already feeling increased as I received the love and attention that was being given to me through Kim's special blessing for my life. I have often felt extremely uncomfortable to be the center of attention and reflected that in the past I would have been deeply embarrassed to be singled out from the group. I had, however, experienced significant growth in my own confidence in the past year and a half as I pursued my life coaching career and discovered that I no longer cringed when I was the center of attention. Instead, I welcomed the love and prayers into my heart. As Joanne led us in song, I gazed out the window at the passing countryside immersed in the sound of our mobile choir.

I listened intently as Linda read Psalm 111, and then Kim read the parable of the prodigal son. Kim's message was direct and easy to follow as she reflected on the message of this familiar parable. It seemed to me that she had selected it with Jeff and Werner in mind, extending the message that God's love and grace is available to everyone, regardless of where they have been in their life. "No matter how far you have strayed from God, He welcomes you back with open arms and embraces you like a long-lost loved one." Kim's voice was loud and strong in its simple message of hope and unconditional love. Once again I found myself drawn to this young pastor. I liked her casual style and her unassuming way of describing God's love and grace to us. Her wide smile was friendly and inviting, while her intense dark eyes riveted my attention.

As she concluded her message she invited me to the front of the bus to assist with Communion. I settled myself into the front seat and handed her the bread to bless and break. I then held each goblet as she filled it with the wine that we purchased the night before. She blessed the wine, and after praying over the elements she explained how we would distribute them. I would start from the back of the bus and she would serve from the front, until we met in the middle. I took half of the bread and a goblet and walked towards the back of the bus, swaying and correcting my gait as we motored down the Autobahn.

The back of the bus was taken up by the Wong family; four Chinese American couples related to one another. Their friendly faces greeted me as I walked unsteadily towards them, balancing bread and wine in each hand. As each person took a piece of the bread I looked into their eyes and gently said, "The body of Christ given for you," and as they dipped it in the goblet of wine I said, "The blood of Christ given for you." Time seemed to stand still as I purposefully prayed for each person taking Communion from me. Some kept their eyes lowered when receiving and some met my gaze with gratitude. I could feel God's love and grace flowing through me as they took the sacraments. I was a messenger in that moment; a conduit for His love and presence.

> I once was lost, but now am found.

Kim did the same from the front of the bus starting with Jeff and working her way back to the middle. When we finished serving the others, Kim and I offered Communion to one another. Joanne led us in a closing song and I smiled even wider as I recognized my favorite hymn, *Amazing Grace*. I closed my eyes and let the words sink in as our voices rose together. It was an unlikely choir and discordant at times, yet I savored the moment. Barreling down the Autobahn, far from home in a foreign land, we were all connected to one another by our belief in Jesus and His universal love.

My heart was overflowing and I silently thanked God yet again for bringing me here. I had no idea it would be this special, this unique, and this fulfilling to travel with my mother, my friends, and my God on a trip to see His Passion. With our church service concluded, I closed my eyes and let the fullness of the experience settle into my being, receiving all that it had offered me. The refrain, "I once was lost, but now am found" reverberated in my mind and I relished how fully found I now felt after years of being lost.

CHAPTER THIRTEEN
REFLECTION QUESTIONS
Discovering Your Story

1. What ceremonies have you participated or assisted in and what was that experience like for you?

2. When have you been lost either physically, mentally, emotionally, or spiritually?

3. In what ways have you been 'found'?

4. What have you found?

CHAPTER *14*

Friendships Old and New

When I sat beside Annemarie at dinner that night she handed me a birthday card with gifts of German chocolate and a bottle of Franciscan red wine. I gratefully hugged and thanked her. She was quickly becoming one of my most favorite people. We chatted about friendships and she told me that she had recently been in touch with a longtime friend of hers, Hilda, who lived near the town of Rothenburg where we now were. She had hoped to be able to see Hilda while in the area, but then sadly explained that Hilda had other commitments and couldn't come to Rothenburg. I could see that Annemarie was disappointed by this news. Patting her hand, I asked her to describe Hilda to me. They had been friends since childhood and had kept in touch through the various phases of their lives. I listened intently as Annemarie described another accomplished and fascinating octogenarian. It was clear to me that Hilda was as interesting a woman as Annemarie, and I was sorry we wouldn't be able to meet her.

Our conversation shifted as we talked with others at our table and enjoyed the meal. Suddenly my eye was drawn to an unfamiliar woman who entered the room and swept her gaze across the dining guests. Annemarie's back was to the door but when this woman saw her, she started to approach our table. Her twinkling eyes caught mine and she motioned for me to keep quiet as she tiptoed forward to surprise Annemarie. It was clearly Hilda, who had gotten away from her other commitments in time to drive to town to meet us. Annemarie was at first startled and then delighted when Hilda tapped her on the shoulder. "Ohhh my gootness!" Annemarie said in amazement. "I can't believe you are here!" Hilda only spoke a little English and she nodded hello as Annemarie introduced her to everyone at the table. We scooted over on the bench to make room for her to join us. They were lifelong friends and it was apparent how dear they were to one another. Spoken language isn't necessary to recognize when love exists. They put their heads together and quietly talked in German while we finished our meal.

After dinner Pastor Kim stood and tapped her glass to get everyone's attention. As she did so, Linda produced a small pastry cake with a single candle in it, much to my surprise and delight. She set the log style cake in front of me while Kim led everyone in singing Happy Birthday. I blew out the candle to a round of applause and congratulations.

As we were enjoying the cake and talking amongst ourselves Jeff suddenly appeared and leaned over me. "Here is how we say Happy Birthday in Germany, Carol," and he planted three alternating kisses on my cheeks in an altogether European fashion. I was enchanted and grinned at his gallantry. He sat down beside me on the bench and asked, "Are you having a good day?" and I replied, "Yes," with a big smile. We chatted about the day, the town's history, and confessed our mutual dislike of glockenspiels while finishing our dessert.

I was enjoying my new friendship with Jeff. We had a relaxed way of conversing and often caught each other's eye with a shared sense-of-humor when something occurred that amused us. More often than not when our tour group walked through the various towns, he and I would fall into step together and engage in easy banter. I found myself increasingly drawn to him as the week progressed.

On one particular day, when we had some free time in town, I struck out on my own for a bit. Wandering up a narrow cobblestoned street, I was content taking in the many sights and sounds of the marketplace. I had no interest in shopping until I noticed a couple of women from our tour group coming out of a store. I paused to say hello and they happily told me about an impromptu wine tasting they had just experienced.

They showed me a small box containing three bottles of their now favorite regional wines. I was interested in tasting the local wine so I waved good-bye as they went on their way and stepped into the store to greet the owner. It was cool and dark inside and as my eyes adjusted to the light I thought, *Now this is shopping I will enjoy!*

At that moment Jeff popped his head in the door of the shop and I smiled and told him I was getting ready to taste some of the regional wines. He was in the process of checking on everyone and said he would touch base with me later. I appreciated his care and turned my attention to the task at hand...sampling the fruits of the Rhine region. After a series of tastings I made my purchase; a box of three local wines to take home. As I stepped onto the street Jeff reappeared and asked how I had enjoyed the tasting. As I told him my impressions he offered to carry my box of wine.

We walked together, making easy conversation with one another on this hot summer day. There was something about him that felt so comfortable yet simultaneously caused my heart to beat faster. It was a feeling I hadn't felt in a long time and I recognized I was enjoying a mild flirtation with him. Since he was thoughtfully carrying my purchases, I offered to buy him an ice cream. He declined, saying that he didn't care much for sweets, but insisted I go ahead and get one. As I made my selection I was aware of his presence beside me and realized I hadn't felt so carefree and open with a man in a very long time. Was it something about Jeff, or travel itself, that made me feel this way? I wasn't sure and I didn't want to over think it. I just wanted to enjoy it.

During our walking connections, Jeff and I talked about all sorts of things from the cooking of a sheep's head (a delicacy in Germany) to the fanciful paintings on the front of the green, yellow and salmon-colored buildings that we often saw. He was full of information and was happy to share it, and I was interested in learning whatever I could about the local culture. In addition to teaching, he was also thoughtful, and I appreciated his caring attention to my mom and Annemarie. His droll sense of humor kept us laughing most days. He teasingly dubbed Linda and me the *Late-ies*, as we had earned a reputation for usually being the last ones to arrive whenever he designated a time for the group to meet.

Despite his teasing, Jeff seemed to understand the challenges of being independent people who were traveling with a group. Balancing my desire to go off and do my own thing while being communicative and responsible to my fellow travelers was a daily issue for me. I felt that he got me in many ways and I appreciated the unexpected newfound friendship with this charming British man. The inner child and flirtatious woman in me, both of which had been dormant for years, seemed to be awakening on this trip. As Jeff and I gravitated towards one another, I recognized the excitement and thrill of connection and attraction that is part of the chemistry that can occur between two people.

Others noticed this chemistry, too, and Linda questioned me about it. "What's up with you and Jeff?"

"I don't know," I responded. "I just really like hanging out with him."

"Yeah, well *something's* going on!" was her reply.

"I know. I don't know what it is. I want to just enjoy it and not try to figure it out," I said. I could tell Linda was not only curious but slightly put out by the time and attention I was spending with Jeff; time that I wasn't available to hang out with her. I felt torn between being with my friend and my curiosity to see what this reconnection with my heart would bring. Linda tried to understand and accept that I was working through lots of new feelings but it wasn't easy for her and she struggled with loneliness at times. Fortunately the older women in our little pod had adopted her as one of their own and she didn't lack for plenty of motherly attention. Their love and care for her was another one of the blessings of the trip, and I was grateful to see deep ties forming between these special women in my life.

On a brief stop at beautiful Neuschwanstein castle (after which the Disney castle is modeled) I took some time by myself to wander through the quaint streets; stopping into shops to select souvenirs for family members at home. When I headed back to the bus to rejoin our group at the appointed time, I rounded the corner to the parking lot, and I saw Jeff and Linda walking towards me.

Jeff was saying to Linda, "Where is Carol? She's gone missing again!"

I heard Linda reply defensively, "She wasn't with me. I don't know where she is."

As they both looked up and saw me at the same time, I sheepishly realized that once again I was going to be the last one to board the bus. I glanced at my watch and saw that I was exactly on time and not a minute late. Unfortunately for me, however, everyone else was already seated on the bus and ready to go. Jeff was out looking for me and dragging Linda along. Feeling defensive, I exclaimed, "Don't tell me I'm the last one again! I'm not even late!"

Linda said with humor, "Ha! It's not me making us late. See it's you!" Jeff's worried look evaporated in a smile as he was clearly relieved to have all his charges accounted for again.

I bantered with Linda saying, "I'm not going to be the last one. I'll race you to the bus," and I took off running across the gravel parking lot. Caught unawares by my unexpected and playful challenge, she shouted, "No fair!" and had a delayed start. I laughed out loud at the sheer joy of racing my friend to the bus. I arrived first and climbed aboard plunking myself down in a seat while catching my breath. Linda plopped down beside me, also out of breath, and we laughed together like children.

A few of our fellow travelers turned towards us and raised their eyebrows at our shenanigans but we didn't care.

It felt great to be alive and merrily engaged in life. I continued to experience a new level of joyfulness on this trip; feeling more carefree than I had in a very long time. What was it that brought this lightheartedness to the surface? I wasn't sure but I was certain that I liked it. Jeff boarded the bus behind us, smiling and shaking his head at our antics, but also clearly appreciating our playfulness.

This journey was bringing unforeseen growth in my relationships with Linda, Mom, Annemarie, and now Jeff. I could never have imagined this experience would evoke such a wide and wonderful array of emotions.

CHAPTER FOURTEEN
REFLECTION QUESTIONS
Discovering Friendship

1. What friendships in your life have been long-lasting?

2. Which ones have been especially fun and joyful?

3. What circumstances have reawakened a dormant side of yourself, such as your inner child, your inner flirt, or another hidden part of you?

CHAPTER *15*

Ich Liebe Dich

Sophie was a tall, thin, brunette woman who was our local tour guide in Würzburg. She had an easy way about her and I liked her immediately. Her eyes were friendly and her German-accented English was easy to follow. Although she was our tour guide for just a day, she taught us a phrase that left an everlasting impression on me.

We began our tour by walking through a deep stone tunnel and emerging within the grounds of Marienberg Fortress; which dates back to the 13th century. As we climbed a gravel path within the fortress, Sophie began telling us about the history of this place where princes and bishops had dwelt. She had lived in Würzburg her entire life, and it was clear how much she loved the city as she enthusiastically shared details about it with us.

Würzburg had been the center of German religious life and had no military significance whatsoever. It saddened me to hear that the Allied forces had bombed it during World War II as a demoralizing tactic. Much of the city was destroyed and had to be rebuilt. Sophie managed to convey this bit of history without judgment. By focusing on reporting the facts and the subsequent rebuilding of Würzberg, she skillfully avoided the emotionally charged controversy of our nationalities that were once at war with each other. She was clearly proud of the fact that subsequent generations, including her own, had worked hard to restore the city back to its previous beauty. I was impressed by her frank and transparent articulation of what were deeply emotional issues. I wondered what God thought about the course of human history and our endless warring for religious reasons.

As we entered through the thick walls of the fortress and continued climbing, I lingered beside Mom to offer an arm of assistance. It was a significant endeavor for her but she leaned on my arm and steadily persisted forward, never once complaining. Whenever she needed to, she would pause to catch her breath and grab an arm for support. She had a healthy balance of being independent as well as comfortably interdependent and willing to receive help. What a great example she was to all of us who can get caught up in the feeling that we need to be constantly self-sufficient. I was impressed by her determination to be here and to get all she could out of this trip. She was remarkable in both her perseverance and her humble acceptance of help from this community of travelers.

After we visited the fortress we returned to our bus for a tour of the rest of the city. Sophie took a position at the head of the aisle and bringing the microphone to her lips she asked, "Well, tell me, now that you've been in Germany for four days, what have you learned to say in our language?"

We began calling out the words we had learned: *guten tag, guten morgan, auf Wiedersehen, bitte/danke, ja, nein.* Sophie nodded her head in approval and then said "Good, good, but have you learned the most important phrase of all?"

We laughed and said, "What? Where is the water closet? Is that the most important thing to know how to say?"

She shook her head good naturedly and said, "I will teach it to you. Are you ready?"

We nodded and shouted our affirmations. "Say it with me," she said, *"Ich liebe dich."* We all mimicked her words, repeating it exactly as she instructed and then asked her what it meant.

Sophie replied, "It means 'I love you' in German. It's the most important phrase to learn because Germans love with their whole hearts. They love their country, their sausage, their beer and one another. So you must know how to say this important phrase if you are in Germany." I smiled in delight learning this new information and practiced saying it over and over again until I got it right. I looked around to see who I could say it to and my gaze landed on my mother.

I called across the aisle to her, "Mom, ich liebe dich," and she turned and smiled at me. Mom is rather unassuming and doesn't like to be the center of attention. I could see, however, that she was delighted in my proclamation of love for her from across the bus. I felt a warm and playful connection with her as I practiced my new German language skills on her. I said the phrase to Bobby and to Linda and to Mom again, getting used to the sound of it rolling off my tongue. Sophie had given me a wonderful parting gift by teaching us this sweet and meaningful phrase before fondly bidding us auf wiedersehen.

―――――――

Later, as I sat beside Annemarie at dinner, our conversation once again turned to my German lessons. I asked her to help me with my pronunciation of ich liebe dich and she corrected and re-corrected me as I tried to mimic the throaty sounds she made. The others at the table laughed at my light-hearted attempts to imitate her sounds without spitting across the table, and also at Annemarie's mock seriousness as she tried to instruct me. As I playfully repeated the phrase to others, she rolled her eyes at me and said, "Ca*rrrr*ol, you have to understand that you don't say this to just anyone, you know."

"What do you mean?" I asked.

"Well, you wouldn't say 'ich liebe dich' to a bus driver. You would save it for someone special," she said.

"I don't know. I think Werner is something special. Don't you think he has done a fabulous job driving us this week through all these tight spaces? I love him for taking such good care of us," I said rather flippantly.

Annemarie gave me a stern look and said emphatically, "No, you don't tell the bus driver that you love him!" I smiled at her grandmotherly scolding and good-naturedly nodded my head in understanding. She continued her lesson. "If you want to tell someone you love them, try this, "'Ich liebe dich, mutter.'" I asked her what that meant and she said, "'I love you, mother' or you could say, 'Ich liebe dich, mutti' to make it even sveeter."

I gave it a shot and rolled it off my tongue "Ich liebe dich, mutti."

"Ja, that is gut!" Annemarie said with a nod of approval and patted my hand. "You got it now." I tried it a few more times casting the words across the table to my mother, who was watching this exchange with great amusement. In fact, we were entertaining the entire table with our German lesson.

Annemarie said, "And your mother would say to you, 'Ich liebe dich, tochter.'" I could tell that Mom wasn't inclined to attempt it with an audience watching so I continued to ask Annemarie how to pronounce various words we had been using all week. She took her role as an instructor very seriously, but also knew how to interject humor and make it fun for all of us. Joanne and Linda joined in the lesson rolling their *r*'s and making guttural sounds in their throats to mimic Annemarie along with me. We entertained one another as we boisterously practiced our German and submitted to her patient corrections.

———————————

My adoption of the 'ich liebe dich' phrase was not only fun but also led to one of the most touching moments of the trip. On an excursion in Zermatt, Switzerland to view the Matterhorn we rode a cog railway slowly up the steep mountain slope. The views were magnificent and the heights dizzying as we looked directly down to the valley below. I was awestruck by the grandeur of God's creation in this Alpine region of the world. As we climbed we saw increasing amounts of snow, a delight in the month of July, and we pulled our jackets around us for warmth. At each stop additional people boarded the train, many of whom were dressed in attire to hike on the trails.

Looking out the big picture windows of the train we reveled in the impressive views seeing mountain goats and hawks at every turn. The massive Matterhorn was the central peak in the landscape while lesser Alps presided around it.

When we reached the top of our ride we exited at Switzerland's highest open-air train station and breathed in the thin, crisp air. The top of the Matterhorn was enshrouded with clouds and was hidden from view, but there were other snowcapped mountains surrounding us as far as the eye could see.

A wide trail zigzagged upwards to an observatory and we headed in that direction. Annemarie decided to take the elevator, but Mom made the decision to hike the trail. She was having some difficulty breathing, however, due to the altitude and the steepness of the slope we were climbing. I was conscious of being close by so that she would have an arm to hang onto if needed. Her desire to do things her way was a trademark of her personality. At times this has frustrated me, but in this instance I was proud of her perseverance. We slowly worked our way uphill towards the observatory with Mom taking periodic breaks to catch her breath.

As we climbed, we noticed a small stone chapel to one side of the trail. It looked like it had been there for ages with its worn, gray exterior and simple steeple. Linda ducked inside and I soon followed, leaving Mom standing outside with Bobby to catch her breath. The interior of the chapel was simple with ten short rows of wooden pews. Candles were glowing on the altar, and I saw that Linda was lighting one and saying a prayer. I moved to the front pew and sat down to absorb the hallowed energy of this place. The burning candles warmed the room and the comforting scent of wax permeated the air. A glow emanated from the altar which felt more potent than just the candles and I sensed that this was a holy place.

I had read that four of the original group which first scaled the Matterhorn in 1865 fell tragically to their death upon their descent. I wondered how many people had visited this small Alpine chapel over the years, and had prayed for those who attempted to climb the surrounding peaks. I basked in the presence of God before lighting a candle.

Afterwards, when I stepped outside I noticed my mother standing by herself and admiring the view. Bobby had wandered off to look over another ridge. I approached Mom and asked if she had seen the chapel. She replied, "Yes, I peeked inside."

"It's really nice in there. Why don't you come with me and sit inside?" I asked. She agreed and took my arm as we ducked our heads and went through the small entranceway. The cozy warmth and hushed atmosphere immediately enveloped us. We slipped into the back pew and sat quietly side-by-side, letting our eyes adjust to the dim lighting and enjoying a respite from the bright, cold day. We gazed at the altar and felt the radiant glow of the lit candles on our faces.

After a while, I leaned over and whispered to her with a smile, "I feel like we're on top of the world." My heart was full of love for her and appreciation to be in this special place together. This trip had been such a blessing for our relationship and I was thankful not only to her, but also to God, for bringing us here. She leaned her curly gray head against mine and we sat like that, steepled in a head-hug, for a few

minutes, and then she whispered "Ich liebe dich, tochter."
It was the first time she had told me, "I love you, daughter"
in German and my eyes misted over with tenderness. It was
the most precious moment of the entire trip, sitting on top of
the world with my mom in this warm chapel, sheltered from
the wind, and hearing her words of love for me.

I tenderly replied, "Ich liebe dich, mutti."

In that cherished moment, I felt the cumulative gift of
unconditional love that my mom and God have always offered
me, but which I haven't always been able to receive. I felt
deeply grateful for the expansion my heart was experiencing
on this journey and my increasing ability to fully accept and
trust the love being presented to me.

CHAPTER FIFTEEN
REFLECTION QUESTIONS
Discovering Unconditional Love

1. In what relationships have you experienced unconditional love?

2. What helps you to recognize and trust unconditional love?

3. What experiences of declaring your love for others have warmed your heart?

4. In what circumstances do you feel most fully engaged in life and grateful to be alive?

CHAPTER 16

The Church in the Meadow

The rolling comfort of the bus and the melodic tones of Jeff's voice lulled me into a quiet, restful state as I only half listened to what he was telling us about our next destination. He was explaining that Wieskirche, commonly known as The Church in the Meadow, was also called The Pilgrimage Church of Wies. It was built in the 1700's after a statue of Jesus was reported to have wept tears on the site. I soon nodded off and awoke sometime later as the bus slowed down and turned into the entrance to Wieskirche.

As usual, Werner negotiated the large tour bus into line beside the others already parked there while Jeff told us that we had forty-five minutes to visit the area. I stepped off the bus and while waiting for the others, I gazed at the church before me. We had seen so many churches by this point on our trip that my first impression was that this one seemed like just another large, impressive house of worship. The major difference being that it was in the middle of a field instead of centrally located in a town or city. I saw a narrow lane leading up to the church that was flanked on one side with vendor booths selling their wares and on the other side with a horse pasture. There was a small restaurant just outside the front doors that was available for simple dining. I had heard about this place from other travelers, but didn't have any great expectations surrounding my visit here…just some curiosity.

Linda and I joined the long line of tourists moving sluggishly towards the entrance. Progress was slow, but we enjoyed looking at the farmland and petting the horses that hung their heads over the fencing beside the lane. When we reached the entrance, the church seemed to tower majestically over us like a grand dame. It seemed out of place here in the farmlands of Bavaria. I climbed the steps, feeling tightly sandwiched between people. As I entered the church my first impression was the height of the ornately painted ceiling which loomed above me. The beauty of the place took my breath away. My eyes widened in awe at the extravagant white and gold decorations adorning the altar and the multitude of frescos on the walls and ceiling.

Within moments of entering I realized that I was feeling a powerful and tangible presence of God. The long line of tourists continued to move slowly around the sides of the sanctuary; some were snapping pictures and others were talking animatedly about the magnificent artwork. Feeling the need to get away from the crowd, I quickly slipped out of line and headed down the center aisle. Something strange was happening to me and I didn't know what it was.

I gravitated towards a roped off area near the front. A sign on a red velvet cord indicated in English *This area reserved for prayer*. I gratefully stepped into this welcoming space and sank into a pew, closing my eyes. I couldn't breathe normally and needed to sit and concentrate on what was happening. The hard wooden pew felt solid beneath me, and by shutting my eyes, I eliminated the distractions of my surroundings. I consciously drew my breath in slowly and deeply, feeling God's very presence in the room. I had only felt this way once before...when I visited the replica of the Grotto of Lourdes near my home with Linda. I was calm and unafraid, yet intensely focused on nothing more than breathing in the spirit of God in this place.

I sensed someone sit down beside me as the wooden bench creaked and opened my eyes slightly to see that it was Linda. Relieved to see my friend, I looked into her eyes with some trepidation and whispered, "It's happening again. I can hardly breathe." I lay my hand on my chest as I struggled to take a deep breath and continued, "His presence is *so* intense here."

Linda replied, "I figured as much. I saw you breathing strangely as soon as we entered."

Seeing the concern in her eyes I said reassuringly, "You can walk around if you want to. I just need to sit here for a while."

"I'll stay with you for a bit," was her reply. I closed my eyes again, comforted by her company.

Experiencing God intensely, I entered a deeply meditative state. My breaths were long, slow and measured; traveling in through my nose and down the back of my throat, swirling through my chest and diaphragm. I filled my lungs slowly with this holy air and exhaled just as slowly. I felt as if every single molecule of air entering my body was charged with a Divine energy. The air was heavy and full of energy. In those sacred moments I knew that God was with me, and everyone, in this church. I was focused entirely on the spirit of God that was both in and around me. Nothing else existed in those moments as my rib cage expanded and contracted with keenly sensitive and spiritual breathing. With my eyes shut I directed my attention inward. All of my other senses must have receded because I was no longer aware of hearing or feeling anything other than my breathing. My mind was empty. The rest of the world grew distant as I concentrated solely on this one thing. In this profoundly meditative state I felt the pure essence of God in the transfer of breath in and out of my body.

I don't know how long I sat there experiencing God's presence so intimately. It was as if time stood still and everything dropped away from my awareness, leaving only

Him and me swirling together in the very air I breathed. My spirit was in contact with the Spirit of God in those sacred moments. I knew I had found a treasure inside of me unlike anything I had ever experienced before.

After some time my sense of hearing began to return and I gradually became aware of the presence of others in the room. It was as if I were approaching the room from a distance; with the sounds growing louder as I drew closer. Keeping my eyes closed, I heard the shuffling of the crowd moving respectfully around the outside of the pews. Gradually the sounds became clearer as if my ears were fine tuning a radio dial. I could still sense Linda beside me on the hard wooden pew and was again comforted by her faithful presence. I slowly opened my eyes, staring first at the floor and then at the surface of the pew directly in front of me. I noticed the grain of the dark polished wood and felt securely hemmed in by the narrow pews before and behind me. As my senses of hearing and sight reconnected with one another and with my surroundings, I slowly became aware of the roomful of people who were oblivious of my experience. It seemed that Linda was the only one who sensed that something powerful had happened to me.

I felt somewhat detached from everyone else; as if returning from a trip and observing and assessing all that was going on around me from a distance. I held onto the edges of the pew on either side of me; grounding myself in their solid form and feeling the stability they offered. I moved slowly as if in a drugged state, lingering in awe at the experience I just had…not wanting it to end.

I raised my head and once again took in the splendor of the stunningly ornate sanctuary. Its beauty was truly breathtaking. My sense of smell had now returned also and I noticed the aroma of wax from the multitude of lit candles in all the alcoves throughout the church. Seeing the flickering candles I was prompted into action. I arose and indicated to Linda that I was going to wander around a bit. We exited the prayer area and went our separate ways to explore this beautiful space.

On either side of the main altar there were narrow passageways with side altars where visitors had lit candles and left prayer requests. Each altar was overflowing with notes and objects of significance that people had left in supplication. As I drew closer to the candles, I could feel on my face the heat that they generated. I was humbled at the sight of so many silent pleas for God's help, and continued to feel an intensity here unlike anything I have ever felt before. The appeals for God's grace and mercy were unspoken yet tangible. As these thoughts settled in I felt a vibration of energy in the room that was unearthly. The energy filled the space up to the vaulted frescoed ceiling and around the wide, concave walls. I lit a candle in honor of this holy place and for all who had stopped to pray here…opening my heart even further. After doing so I wandered around the edges of the sanctuary, savoring the prayerful spirit of the place before slowly exiting. I felt as if I were in a slightly surreal stupor.

Stepping out of the church, the day was still bright and sunny outside. It looked the same as when I had arrived 40 minutes earlier, but I felt completely different. I walked down the lane to our bus with a feeling of wonder at my own transformation. I again noticed the vendors selling souvenirs, but I passed by them, lost in my own thoughts while trying to absorb what I had just experienced. Back in the parking lot I noticed Jeff was looking frazzled as he searched for members of our group amongst the vendor stands. As he approached me I had a fleeting worry that I was the last one to be found again. "We're going to be late to the hotel if we don't get going," he fretted, and I hurried to climb aboard the bus.

Once on the bus, I realized that several members of our group were still not present and I was relieved to finally not be the last one on board. As I looked at Jeff and the others I felt oddly disconnected. It appeared to me that they had not been as impacted by this place as I had been. When I spoke to my Mom and Bobby, I felt my face flush with the glow of my experience. While they agreed we had just been to a special place, the look on their faces told me they didn't feel the same excitement that I did. I was grateful that Linda understood.

When we took our seats I could hardly contain my excitement. I leapt to my feet and rushed up the aisle to the front of the bus, tapping Pastor Kim on her shoulder. "Kim, did you feel it?!! Did you feel the energy in that place?" I exclaimed.

I felt as if my face was shining like Moses' when he came down from the mountain top.

Kim turned towards me with tears streaming down her face. "Yes," she whispered, "Oh Carol, yes, I felt it. I don't know what to say. That is surely God's holy place." I hugged her and we smiled into each other's eyes with an understanding that comes from a shared experience which goes beyond words. I returned to my seat and wrapped my arms around myself with suppressed excitement. I didn't know what it meant, but I knew something amazing had just happened to me. My eyes shone as I stared out the window at the beautiful Church in the Meadow as we drove away.

I was slightly disappointed that others didn't identify with my intense God connection. The joy I felt, however, overshadowed the disappointment of not being understood. I felt incredibly blessed. This trip to Oberammergau was the closest thing to a pilgrimage that I had ever experienced. I had wondered how I would encounter God on the journey. Visiting this holy place and feeling God's presence in such a potent way was an unexpected gift beyond measure. I treasured it in my heart and was curious how the impact of this experience would continue to develop within me.

It would take me months to fully comprehend what happened to me that afternoon. Later I would come to know that God's mighty arm swept away the remaining walls that I had been slowly deconstructing for years. In my mind's eye I envisioned an arc of pure white sand swept clean by the powerful arm of God. The stones of my walls were pushed off to the side and out of sight and I found the lost part of my heart and soul in God's healing breath.

CHAPTER SIXTEEN
REFLECTION QUESTIONS

Discovering Your Spiritual Connections

1. What have been your most powerful connections with God?

2. In what situations have you been surprised by the presence of God?

3. What has been your experience with deeply meditative states? In what ways did these experiences heighten your awareness?

4. What have you learned from your own transformative encounters with God?

5. When given the opportunity to share, what would you want to convey to others about those moments?

CHAPTER *17*

The Passion Play

My search for a deeper connection with God continued to unfold as the day for the Passion Play arrived. We had traveled far, and reaching this destination was the highlight of our journey. As with any special occasion, many of us had dressed up for this long-awaited event. Pastor Kim was clad in a long, flowing, white skirt and white blouse. Some of our group chatted with her while waiting for the time when we would enter the theater. I remarked how pretty she looked and she commented that today was a holy day and she wanted to look her best. Her bright smile declared her joy about finally being here in the village of Oberammergau for the Passion Play. I continued to gravitate to the special energy this young pastor emanated.

As we gathered around Kim and shared our impressions of the village and the anticipation we were feeling as the time for the grand performance drew near, she turned to me and said amiably, "You know, Carol, I had the most interesting dream about you and I've been meaning to tell you about it."

"Really?" I said, and raised my eyebrows inquiringly towards her.

"Yes, I was resting on my bed that first day when we arrived in Boppard and even though I was only half awake I dreamt about you. You were carrying around a baby girl and were showing her to everyone. You were incredibly happy,... joyful, in fact. Everyone was looking at your baby and you were so thrilled with her."

She looked at me expectantly but I wasn't sure what to make of her dream so I put on my life coach role for a moment and said, "I have heard that when we dream, we ourselves are every character in the dream. If that's the case, what does that dream tell you about yourself?"

She looked rather surprised by my observation and said, "Hmm, I don't know. I'll have to think about that." I brushed off the dream as not really having anything to do with me. It would have more significance later, however, and I would find myself talking with her about it once we returned home. For now though, the hour had finally come to see the play.

The theater was a unique building which the village of Oberammergau had built specifically for its performances of The Passion Play, which occurred every ten years. A long rectangular building with large wide doors on the sides, it seated 4700 people. The entrances looked like garage doors, with oversized letters of the alphabet above them indicating where the audience should enter. Checking our tickets, we queued outside the letter N door waiting for it to roll open precisely at 2:00 PM for this sold out performance.

As I was talking to Linda and Mom a man walked by just a few feet away from us who looked like someone I knew. I shook my head in startled surprise and thought I must be mistaken. Running into someone I knew so far from home in another country in the midst of such a large crowd was incomprehensible to me. I tentatively said his name out loud, "Greg?" I fully expected the man to turn towards me and I would see that it was a stranger. Then I would apologize to him saying, "Sorry, you look like someone I know."

The man stopped in his tracks, however, and turned to me and said, "Carol?" with equal surprise and wonder. It *was* Greg! I felt an instant connection and flew into his arms for a big bear hug. There was a timeless quality to that moment and in it I realized *it felt like home to me*. The sudden and unexpected warmth of his embrace felt surprisingly safe, and my heart leapt inside of me in recognition of something it was longing for. I sensed a remarkable bond between us even as my mind struggled to comprehend this unexpected encounter.

We both spoke at once asking, "What are you doing here?" as we released each other from our spontaneous hug. He replied first and explained that he was traveling with his church on a tour through Germany to see the Passion Play. I briefly described how I came to be there and shook my head in wonder saying, "I can't believe we ran into each other here, what are the odds of that?!"

I turned and saw the dumbfounded expressions on the faces of our companions who were witnessing all that just took place and were looking as surprised as Greg and I were. We introduced each other to our traveling buddies and then proceeded to talk about the places we had been and our expectations of the play. As we did so, I continued to gaze in amazement at Greg... trying to comprehend this synchronistic meeting. In those brief moments I savored the feeling of home I had just had with Greg; which connected me to my country, my home town, my church-family, and God.

Greg also knows my friend Pat, who often runs into people she knows when she is traveling far from home. I like to tease Pat about her uncanny ability to find familiar faces in distant places. Greg and I agreed that Pat would appreciate our chance meeting and we each looked forward to telling her about it when we returned home. My encounter with Greg was brief, but it warmed my heart and made a lasting impression.

As the doors to the theater opened Greg and I said good-bye and wished each other well. I walked away still shaking my head at the wonder of it all. As we moved to our seats I explained to my curious traveling companions that Greg was a man I knew from years ago at my previous church. He and his wife Lori were one of the couples that Matt and I were acquainted with when we were married. When Matt and I separated, I changed churches and had lost touch with Greg and Lori except for occasionally running into Lori around town at business networking events.

Tragically, Greg had lost Lori in an automobile accident a year and a half earlier. The last time I had seen him was when I attended her memorial service. I marveled at the unexpected appearance of him in this immense crowd. I knew instinctively that God had provided this serendipitous encounter…even though I didn't know why.

Once inside the open-air theater we took our seats, which we happily realized were centrally located and only twelve rows from the stage. The play was to be performed in two Acts with a break in between the Acts for dinner and wandering about town. It would be performed in German, so we had each been given a program booklet that contained the English translation.

The set was simply designed with pillars and archways that were typical of Roman architecture during Biblical times. The stage itself was huge, and the absence of the ceiling which revealed the blue sky above with clouds drifting by made it seem even larger. The theatre backdrop was the Bavarian foothills surrounding the village of Oberammergau. There was a soft summer breeze blowing through the theater and an air of anticipation in the entire audience.

The full orchestra announced the beginning of the play while hundreds of villagers of all ages poured onto the stage waving palm fronds, heralding Jesus' entrance into Jerusalem. The ensemble included young children as well as real sheep and goats, and even a camel. All of the villagers were dressed in simple teal-colored robes with scarves or turbans of the same color wrapped around their heads. The enthusiasm of the crowds welcoming Jesus was electrifying.

Jesus entered on a live donkey and was smiling at the crowds. He was a ruggedly attractive man in his thirties with long brown hair. His disciples walked alongside of his donkey. They were also men with long hair and were dressed in simple khaki-colored linen robes, as was Jesus. The villagers that represented the Jewish religious leaders wore robes of varying colors and were distinguished by rather large, oblong hats, which had an almost science-fiction appearance to them. These leaders looked pensive as they analyzed the situation that was unfolding before them. There was a foreboding among these leaders at the beginning of the play, and you could almost hear what they were thinking above the joyous shouts of the crowds and the brass, strings and drums from the orchestra. *This Jesus has a large and devoted following that is growing in numbers by the day, and now he has come to this holy city of Jerusalem.*

When Jesus dismounted from his donkey and spoke to the crowds, he did so in German. We had been told that we would not need to read the programs since the story of the Passion was so familiar, but once the play started I found that I wanted to know exactly what they were saying. I propped the booklet against the seat in front of me so that I could glance down at it, scan a few lines at a time and then look back at the stage to watch the performers. In that way I figured out who was who and I could interpret the dialogue.

Linda and I were engrossed in following the performance with our programs. I glanced over at my mom to see how she was enjoying the play and saw that she was nodding off. The day was very warm and we were sitting in the sun. I shook my head and chuckled to myself that she had come so far to see this once-in-a-lifetime performance and was now too sleepy to watch it.

I returned my attention to the play and thoroughly enjoyed each unfolding scene as the afternoon flew by. Since it was a musical, there were intervals when the chorus would gather together to sing. These were all adult men and women dressed in long white robes with gray turban-like headdresses. I was pleased to see that the beauty and passion of the story were clearly conveyed in a foreign language. All of the performers expressed such deep emotion that I found it hard to believe that these were just ordinary villagers and not professionals.

When we broke for intermission we filed out of our row into the bright afternoon sunshine. It felt good to stretch our legs and walk around and we talked excitedly about the play. We saw Jeff holding a sign with the name of our tour group on it and we made our way over to him through the large crowd. He led us back to the restaurant where we had eaten lunch, and we comfortably settled ourselves for dinner.

Once seated, I glanced over my shoulder and noticed Jeff sitting alone and invited him to join our table. The others looked a bit surprised as it required them to scoot over on the long bench on one side of the table to make room for Jeff at the end. I said, "No one should eat alone," and they quickly agreed and shifted seats in accommodation.

Jeff situated himself beside me and asked how I was enjoying the play. I told him how much I liked it and we chatted amiably about the language differences and the challenges of the translation material. "Have you ever seen the play?" I asked.

"No, they don't give tickets to the tour guides. I've been here several times this summer but haven't actually seen the play," was his reply.

"That's too bad. I think you would enjoy it. It seems unfair to come here and not be able to see it. If you ever get the chance I hope you'll do it," I said, while Jeff looked at me thoughtfully.

When our meal was finished, we had some free time before the second act. A few of us chose to wander through the town museum to learn more about Oberammergau's history. We happened upon an actor dressed in character who was engaging visitors in conversation. Curious, we paused to listen and ask a few questions. He informed us that he was one of Herod's guards in that day's performance. Someone commented about his long bushy beard and he explained that the village men were required to grow their facial hair for an entire year before the performance to lend authenticity to their role. I was impressed yet again by the dedication of these local townspeople to participate in a production of this size.

He went on to say that there are 5,000 residents in the village and 2,500 of them participate in the play in one way or another. There is a full orchestra, a choir, and a large cast of up to 1,000 people and animals on the stage at one time. The sheer size of the performance, in addition to how long the tradition has continued, was incredibly impressive to me. As he spoke, more people gathered to hear him explain that performers have to be residents of the village for twenty years before they are allowed to participate in the play.

We were so absorbed in the details of his explanation that we lost track of time. Suddenly realizing that the intermission was almost over, we said to him, "You must need to be going soon to get ready for the second act." He was very calm, however, and finished having his picture taken with some of us before heading to the theater. As we returned to our seats, we heard someone remark that the actress who played Mary was also the owner of the shop where she had made purchases during intermission. Seeing how the play was so intimately integrated into the life of these villagers and observing their casual attitude just added to our sense of wonder about this entire experience.

As we approached the theater I saw Greg leaning with his foot on a low fence railing, talking with people from his tour group. I thought about going over to chat with them again, but decided it was more important to stay with my own group and get settled into my seat. I smiled inwardly, still astonished that I had run into him here.

The second half of the production was easier to follow without reading as much of the translation as I had during the first half of the show. Mom was more wakeful in the cooler evening air and I shared my translation booklet with her. She had taken the advice of those who said she wouldn't need the program and had left hers at the hotel. She regretted that decision in hindsight and appreciated being able to interpret some of the dialogue with the help of the booklet.

As the light of day faded we pulled out small flashlights that we had brought to illuminate the words. Darkness gradually settled onto the natural backdrop of the stage and soon the mountains faded from view. Eventually, the passionate performances and captivating story compelled me to close the booklet entirely, and I experienced the remainder of the play without verbal translation.

The actor who played Judas Iscariot was stellar in his performance. His interpretation of Judas's torment upon realizing the consequences of his betrayal of Jesus was powerful. I was especially affected by how Peter and Judas each handled the realization that they had betrayed Christ. No interpretation was necessary when both of these disciples expressed the heart-wrenching torment they each felt over their betrayal and denial of Jesus.

I was awestruck by the closing scene of the crucifixion. Although I knew intellectually that there were props being used to nail Jesus to the cross, the scene was incredibly convincing. The three crosses were hoisted upward by ropes, with Jesus and each of the two thieves hanging on them. The sky was now completely dark. Sitting in the theater on that balmy summer night in Germany and witnessing the final crucifixion scene of the Passion Play, I was left speechless by the unfathomable love that God has for us. I found comfort and hope in the final scene when the resurrected Christ appeared in flowing white robes and stood beneath a tree with a crowd of followers surrounding him; all of them holding lit candles. It was made clear that the light of God's love continues in each of us.

As we left the theater our group walked sedately in quiet contemplation. I fell into step beside my mother and wrapped a loving arm around her shoulder. "Thank you," I said, as I looked into her eyes with genuine appreciation. Deep gratitude welled inside me for her gift of sharing this unique expression of the passion of Jesus with me. Her eyes were moist as she wrapped her arm around my waist, gazed into my eyes, and sincerely said, "You're welcome."

God had surely moved through this compelling performance and I felt both humbled and blessed to have witnessed it.

CHAPTER SEVENTEEN
REFLECTION QUESTIONS
Discovering Serendipity

1. What are your observations about coincidences or serendipitous occurrences? What significance do you give to them?

2. What would it be like to believe in divinely orchestrated appointments?

3. What performances have had a powerful impact on you?

4. What experiences have you had with the story of the Passion of Christ? What emotions has the story evoked in you?

5. Who, or what, in your life feels like home to you? Describe what that feels like.

CHAPTER 18

Peter and Judas

As our bus left Oberammergau the morning after the play, Pastor Kim took the microphone to give us her gold nugget of the day. By this point in the trip, I eagerly anticipated her morning insights and her daily reading of a Bible passage, and her short reflection afterwards always gave me something interesting to contemplate. On this day Kim shared her impressions of the Passion Play and we listened intently. She then invited anyone else who wanted to speak to come forward. I looked around the bus to see if anyone was getting up, but no one was rising from their seat. Then, prompted by an inner nudge from the Holy Spirit, I knew I had something to say. I hesitated briefly and then rose to work my way down the aisle, steadying myself on the seat backs as the bus motored along the highway. I made eye contact with Kim and her look of encouragement calmed the butterflies I had in my stomach. Speaking in front of a group used to be very difficult for me, but I have learned to trust that God will help me express myself.

Normally, when I speak publicly, I prepare my thoughts in advance accompanied by notes to guide me. It was out of character for me to speak off-the-cuff and I surprised myself by even having the courage to step forward. Saying a silent breath prayer to ask God to bless my words, I took the microphone from Kim. I braced myself and faced the busload of my fellow travelers. I could see their faces peaking around the high backed seats in order to see me. Aware that I had their full attention, I prefaced my comments by saying, "Like many of us, I am still absorbing the impact of yesterday's play. I will share with you what I'm thinking so far, though, and hope it's of interest."

I began, "The play had a powerful effect on me and while it was a familiar story there are a couple of points that have taken on new meanings as I ponder them. I was impacted most by the performances of the actors who portrayed Judas and Peter. Their interpretation gave me a new awareness of the torment the disciples must have felt when they realized how they had betrayed Christ." The curious expressions on the faces before me encouraged me to continue with my impressions of these characters.

"It was clear to me that initially Judas was trying to help. He wanted circumstances to go better for the cause of the disciples and took the situation into his own hands to try to make it happen. I personally can relate to that, because there are times in my life where I do the same thing. I think I know a better or faster way to get the results that I deem necessary. I am guilty of the same pitfalls as Judas. Seeking control, I take things into my own hands and direct the course to an outcome I've created in my mind. I disregard the signs before me and plow ahead with a single-minded purpose to do it my own way. Jesus knew Judas would betray him and even predicted it out loud, but Judas did it anyway, thinking that he knew better than Christ. How often do I do the same?" I had the attention of my fellow travelers and many were nodding their heads in agreement now.

I continued, "When Judas realized the full impact of what he had done, he was overwhelmed with torment and grief. He never intended for it to go the way it did. He led the guards to Jesus in the garden and kissed him on the cheek to identify that this was the man they should arrest. He carried out his part of the plan and it wasn't until hours later when he saw the guards scourging Jesus that he realized the mistake he had made.

"How often am I like Judas and only see what I have done in hindsight? As I watched Judas cry out in agony over his crucial error and witnessed his tormented mind and crushing regret, I was struck by his self-hatred. He ran away in agony and tore his clothes in grief, realizing he had betrayed the one he loved, despite his good intentions. By taking matters into his own hands he led Jesus to the cross. Seeing how his actions betrayed the one he loved, Judas went over a mental edge into self-loathing that was personally devastating. He could not forgive himself and took his own life.

"And then we have Peter, who also betrayed Jesus in his hour of need. As the events of the evening unfolded, Peter was caught up in the mob mentality and became fearful. His fear caused him to deny Jesus three times, just as Christ said he would. When the rooster crowed and he realized what he had done, he too, was tormented and overcome with grief. Unlike Judas, though, he sought forgiveness. He went to Mary, the mother of Jesus, confessed what he had done, and begged forgiveness. By reaching out to others, speaking of his mistake, and asking for forgiveness, he was able to reconcile his regret and went on to build the Church for Christ.

"Even though the story was familiar, what was different for me as I watched this performance, was that I recognized myself in every character. I try to be like Jesus in my thoughts, words, and deeds. The mother in me relates to the nurturing character of Mary. I recognize myself in the brotherly love of John as well as in Thomas the doubter. I empathize with the womanly love Mary Magdalene had for her Savior. And I can now see myself more in Peter and Judas, who were each lost in their sea of despair and self-loathing. I can learn from them what I must do when I disappoint myself and others. Like Peter, I give into fear but I can ask for forgiveness and try again. Like Judas I try to take control and often forget to trust God's plan. Self-hatred sent Judas over the edge into despair. I have not experienced the depth of torment that Judas did, but I make poor decisions and usually criticize myself when I do.

"The lesson I learned from Judas' and Peter's behaviors is to now honestly ask myself: How do I handle the consequences of my mistakes? Do I condemn myself and turn away from God, or do I move towards God with my suffering and seek forgiveness and a relationship grounded in love? Do I search for my sure footing again by asking for, and receiving the grace and compassionate mercy that God offers me?" With that final question, I set the microphone down and took my seat as Kim and my fellow travelers quietly thanked me for my comments.

Another member of the group rose to share his thoughts about the play and I settled into my seat to listen to his perspectives. When he finished Kim closed our reflection time with a prayer. We sang *Amazing Grace* to complete our sharing time and I was touched again by the phrase "I was lost and now I'm found, was blind but now I see." When I've been lost, whether physically, mentally, emotionally or spiritually, I have needed God and those He sent me, to help me find my way again. Realizing how He has provided for me throughout my life, I was filled with gratitude as we sang this old hymn. I discover a profound truth contained within it.

I am not perfect and I struggle as others do. Despite my best efforts, I will at times let myself and others down. Knowing how to love and forgive myself as well as how to ask and receive forgiveness from others is crucial for my personal development. Through a loving relationship with God, and myself, I am able to continue to grow and evolve into the woman I am uniquely designed to be.

CHAPTER EIGHTEEN
REFLECTION QUESTIONS
Discovering Forgiveness

1. What has been your experience with trying to take control and later regretting it?

2. What has helped you acknowledge your regret and made it possible to seek forgiveness?

3. What have you learned about forgiving yourself?

4. We can recognize some of our own traits in the characters of any given story. Who, or what, do you identify with in the Passion story?

5. What has been your experience of being physically, emotionally, mentally or spiritually lost? What helped you through that experience?

CHAPTER *19*

Everyone Has a Story

While existing relationships can be deepened and sometimes tested during travel, new friendships can be an enriching benefit of stepping out of our comfort zone. Whether close to home or across the globe, I thoroughly enjoy talking with new people and getting to know their stories.

Annemarie had taught us that coffee and cake was a wonderful German tradition, much like the English tea, where folks pause for an afternoon break at 4:00 PM to relax and reconnect with one another. Honoring our request to get off the tourist bus route and visit a local German town, Jeff had brought us to a renowned bakery in Ehrsberg to experience coffee and cake.

We stood salivating over the display of pastries and cakes while breathing in the heady aroma of strong coffee and sugar that filled the air. I asked a tall woman behind me for her recommendations about the confections before us. As she spoke I was pleasantly surprised to learn that she was an American. She and her husband had traveled from Denver, Colorado, and were in Germany to celebrate her mother-in-law's ninetieth birthday. After we made our selections I motioned to Linda that I was going to sit with my new acquaintances to continue our conversation and enjoy our pastries. I spent a delightful twenty minutes getting to know Diana and her husband Mark before they went on their way.

Leaving the bakery, Jeff said that he thought it was remarkable that I had run into people I knew in this quaint little town off the beaten track. I said with a smile, "Oh, I didn't know them. I just started talking to them in line and was curious about their story." He seemed surprised at my willingness to converse and sit with strangers, yet smiled and nodded his approval.

I come by this behavior honestly. When my parents were married, they had loved to travel and would frequently strike up conversations with perfect strangers they met along the way. As a teenager, I remember being embarrassed when my father would talk and laugh with the waitresses, and even ask them personal questions, when we were out to dinner. I would blush intensely, draw my shoulders around my ears and visualize sliding under the table to escape. Dad would brush off my discomfort and continue with his custom of being curious about people's lives. He called it "What's your story, Morning Glory?" and just like the flower by that name, when the conditions were right, people would open up and share their stories with him. I have to confess, however, that over the years, my mother and I, as well as some of my siblings, have adopted this same habit.

I had the opportunity over the course of our trip to engage in this habit with Jeff. Our growing friendship and the easy banter we had been experiencing all week was an unforeseen and yet joyful part of my trip. As I had told Linda, I wasn't really thinking about it and just wanted to let it unfold. I could not deny or resist the unexpected pleasure I was experiencing being in Jeff's company. I felt carefree, exhilarated, and flirtatious in his presence; feelings I hadn't sensed in a very long time. I chose not to over-think my attraction to him, or even try to define it. I just accepted it for what it was, which in itself, was a major shift for me. Being accustomed to making things happen in my life, it felt refreshing to release control and instead be completely open and receptive to what God was providing.

Linda had pointed out, "You realize he is nothing that you say you're looking for. He's not taller than you; he smokes, and likes to talk about himself... *a lot!*" Like the good friend that she was, Linda was reminding me of aspects I had told her previously that I wanted in a future partner. Jeff had similar qualities to men in my past relationships, and Linda now saw red flags everywhere. Even though I heard her warnings, I wasn't ready to heed these contradictions yet, and filed them away in some remote part of my brain. I sensed that my budding relationship with Jeff was making Linda uncomfortable on several levels, but was unable to address the situation fully at that time. I wasn't sure what to make of it, but I also trusted that God was providing some lessons for Linda in this experience as well, which we would both come to understand in time.

Jeff's lifestyle was unlike anyone I had ever met before, which made him seem fascinating and eccentric to me. While seated beside me on the bus, he revealed some of his life story. He chose to spend May through October working as a tour guide out of Munich, Germany, and then spent the rest of his year in India. His specialty as a guide was Nazi German history, so he usually provided day tours in the Munich area, sharing his expertise on Hitler and the concentration camps.

I had read Anne Frank's autobiography and had visited her home in Amsterdam as well as the site of Corrie ten Boom's home. Jeff was unfamiliar with Corrie's story, so I explained to him that she was a Christian woman who had helped Jews escape Germany until she and her sister were caught and sent to a concentration camp themselves. Corrie survived but her sister did not. Eventually she told her story of how she held onto hope in desperate times. She inspired thousands by recounting the challenges of forgiving one of the guards who had held her captive many years later.

I was curious to know how Jeff handled presenting such horrific material to clients and asked how he did it. He explained that he sticks to the facts. Remaining factual about the history helps him, and his clients, manage the gruesome information he shares.

Jeff went on to explain that it was unusual for him to do an Oberammergau trip. With a sigh of relief he said, "I'm glad I got it. It seems as if there aren't as many tours scheduled this year as there were in 2000 for the Passion Play. The economy is affecting people's travel budgets. I had one other Oberammergau tour earlier this season, and now this one." I told him that I was glad he took this tour in particular, and that I believed God brought it to him for a reason.

As Werner drove our bus through the towering Swiss Alps, my conversation with Jeff continued and I asked him about India and the family that he mentioned he supports there. "You are quite the provider," I observed, and he gave me a startled look. I continued, "You do a great job of taking care of us on the tour and you are clearly very fond of this family in India." He seemed surprised by my observations, as if no one had ever said that to him before, yet he also seemed appreciative, as he relaxed back into his seat.

"I suppose I am. I have eight people to provide for," he said, somewhat proudly. He counted them off on his fingers, "The family in India, two godchildren, a child in an Indian orphanage, and an ex-wife's child. The child is not my own but I send her money for him anyway. In fact, none of the children are my own. I suppose I have done my life backwards," he reflected. "I spent my younger years traveling and seeing the world, and now that I am older I want a family." His honesty was disarming and I tried to comprehend the extremely different lifestyle which he led that was so unfamiliar to me. He was kind, thoughtful, and honest, with an unusual mixture of responsibility and carefreeness dividing his year between two very different countries. I wondered aloud what it must be like.

"It's great! I work half the year and take the other half off," he said. I, myself, couldn't imagine a lifestyle like that and asked how he spends his time in India. "I lay about for bit," he replied. "I'm thinking of starting a business but it takes a LOT of money. You have to bribe the legal system there to get anything done."

I tried to comprehend working half a year and then playing for the other half. It was a foreign concept to me, yet also strangely enticing. I was certainly enjoying the lack of responsibilities on this trip, but I wondered if I would get bored after some time without my work. I wasn't sure if I liked that insight about myself or not. Knowing that I can get caught up in busyness and the 'doing' of life, I longed for more experiences where I could just *be*. Jeff was providing an example of what that might look like, and I was admittedly intrigued.

I shifted the conversation and asked him what he liked about India. His eyes lit up with excitement as he answered,

"Oh, it's great, Carol! There's always something going on. My absolute favorite thing to do is to take a train ride through India because it's fascinating to see all the people and animals. It's amazing. I never get bored there." It was clear to me that he loved it.

I thought of my sister Sally who had recently been to India. She had described to me the mayhem that occurs on the roads due to a lack of traffic laws. She said it wasn't unusual to see five or more people piling onto one motorcycle. Jeff confirmed that this was true and that there were monkeys and cows everywhere. This caused me to think of other exotic animals and I asked him if he'd ever ridden an elephant. "Sure I have, but it's not all that it's cracked up to be. In fact, it's really rather uncomfortable with your legs spread wide across the back of the elephant and it shifting from side to side as it walks. It's a bit of a rub," he replied, painting an image that did indeed sound uncomfortable. "I wouldn't recommend it," he said, in a droll, understated British tone. I was unconvinced by his description, still thinking that riding an elephant was something I would try if given the opportunity.

I asked what other plans he had going forward. "Well, I'm off to England after this trip on a bit of a holiday. I don't usually take vacations during tour season because I need the work while it's available, but I'm off to visit my Dad and my brother." His British accent grew thicker as he spoke of England. "Me Dad's got it in his mind that we need to take a trip to Scotland, just the three of us, to visit me Mum's homeland. Me Mum's been gone a long time, since I was 19, and me Dad isn't well. This is some sort of last wish of 'is. My brother is a pain and my Dad's a bit dotty, so I don't know how that's going to go. But you do what you need to do, right?" he said, latching me with a quizzical eye.

"After that I'll return to Munich and do more tours until October, and then I'll see about heading back to India." I noted a surprising lack of enthusiasm when he said this as compared to our earlier conversation, and questioned him about it.

Jeff insisted, "Well, I am excited. I'm just not sure about a relationship I have with a woman over there. I'm fond of her but you just know when someone loves you, eh?" I thought to myself that I wasn't at all sure since my own marriage had failed. I decided not to share my cynicism about love, and instead acknowledged how challenging relationships can be. He was clearly weighing the differences in their feelings about each other and I appreciated his honesty.

Our conversation ended as he once again focused his attention on his tour guide duties. Leaning back on the headrest and gazing out the window, I contemplated how we had innocently flirted with each other during this trip. A flood of warmth arose within my heart and I felt grateful for our connection. I was pleased that he entrusted me with his thoughts and feelings about his relationships and lifestyle. Even though I had no idea why this bond had happened between the two of us, I believed God had a reason for it.

As the bus sped along the road I found myself again simply trusting in God's plan. I smiled inwardly, recognizing how far I'd come in my ability to let go of control and to unquestioningly receive the blessings He was giving me.

CHAPTER NINETEEN
REFLECTION QUESTIONS
Discovering
Personal Connections

1. When have you experienced an immediate and genuine connection to someone?

2. In what ways do you see those interactions as part of God's overall plan?

3. How do you practice being fully present?

4. What gets in the way of just *being*?

Rainbow Promises and Goodbyes

A soggy day in Lucerne didn't dampen our spirits as we traipsed around the city in our raincoats. The overcast weather also couldn't diminish the pleasure we took in seeing this beautiful city, which sat on the edge of Lake Lucerne and was surrounded by the Swiss Alps. We were especially enchanted by the medieval Chapel Bridge, considered to be one of the oldest covered wooden bridges in Europe. The bridge provided a pedestrian walkway across the Reuss River. Abundantly overflowing flower baskets lined each side of the bridge, gracing us with their colorful arrays. The pinks and purples of the blossoms were all the more vivid displayed against the backdrop of the gray sky.

The clouds finally broke towards the end of the day, and we shed our raincoats to enjoy the warm evening air. Some of our group had decided to attend a Swiss Folk Dinner Theater that night, while others of us chose to venture out on our own for our last meal in Europe together. The restaurant we selected overlooked the river and the flower-laden Chapel Bridge. Waiters wiped off wet chairs at an outdoor table and we settled down to dine al fresco in this picturesque location. As we were seated we noticed a rainbow forming over the bridge.

Our eyes were drawn across the river, where the setting sun cast its vibrant rays on a stately pink marble church, which emanated a soft rosy glow. The huge rainbow arched across the blue sky, hugging the flower-covered bridge in a colorful embrace. It was breathtakingly beautiful. We tried to capture it with our cameras, but it was a scene that never could have been fully represented in a photo. I took a mental snapshot, savoring the moment, knowing it was God's promise to us all. I interpreted the rainbow as a reminder that He would continue to be with me long after this trip was over. He had moved my heart in ways that I had yet to fully comprehend.

I was filled with a mixture of emotions. Flirtatious, fun feelings for Jeff mingled with grateful, adoring, daughterly love for Mom, Annemarie and Bobby, and a warmhearted sisterly love for Linda. I had received a full spectrum of heart-filling experiences on this trip. What better way to end our last night in Europe than with the fellowship of loved ones, and this symbolic reassurance of God's constant presence.

The only cloud lingering on my emotional horizon was my approaching goodbye with Jeff. A growing uneasiness crept into my heart as our time in Lucerne came to a close, knowing that it would be my last day with this man whom I had grown so fond of. Anticipating the need for some time alone together, Jeff and I had made plans earlier in the day to meet for a nightcap when he returned from the Folk show. Later that evening I left the hotel to meet him. Catching his eye across the plaza, he waved, and we exchanged bright smiles. Even though it was 10:00 PM, the sky was still light. Now free from our responsibilities to others, we were both ready to enjoy some exclusive time together.

As I approached him I offered him the last bottle of wine that I had bought earlier in the trip and said, "Hi! I have a gift for you. I don't want to take this back home with me and was hoping you would take it."

He seemed pleased and said "Sure. Thank you very much!" Having carried the wine through village streets for me, it seemed only fitting that he get the last bottle.

He asked me where I wanted to go and I said, "Somewhere other than the hotel." I wanted to be somewhere cozier and more casual. He smiled in easy agreement and we crossed the street to a sidewalk café. As we settled ourselves at a table he lit a cigarette and ordered two beers for us in German.

We chatted easily about our respective dinner experiences. He told me humorous anecdotes about one of our tour group members who had entered a beer drinking contest during the Folk show, as well as how Pastor Kim had been accosted by a giant Swiss cow as part of the entertainment. We laughed comfortably with each other and then I told him about our dinner and the beautiful rainbow.

As our conversation continued he asked, "What did you enjoy most about the tour?" I shared with him the many aspects that I liked, but concluded with this overall observation, "I have just been incredibly happy on this trip. I loved being with my mom here and feeling so close to her." That was apparent to him and he agreed that my mom was, indeed, a very special lady.

We talked awhile about our parents. Jeff's mother died when he was nineteen, so he spoke mostly about his relationship with his father and brother. I shared a bit about my dad's passing when I was thirty, and we got to know more of each other's history talking about these special people in our lives. Savoring our newfound friendship, we spent a couple of relaxing hours together on our last summer evening in Lucerne. At one point I reached out and absentmindedly rubbed the sleeve of his red windbreaker between my fingers. He looked a little surprised, and self-consciously noticing what I was doing, I stopped and smiled at him. I don't know what it was about Jeff. I felt unusually comfortable with him. He was so easy to be with, and my heart warmed just to catch his eye and to share a smile with him. There was an indescribable chemistry between us.

At midnight the waitress told us they had to close the outdoor section so we moved inside. Stools were lined up at a window bar that looked out into the street. The place was full, but we found one stool and he offered it to me while he stood. He ordered two more drinks for us as we continued talking. By now the conversation had turned to spiritual matters and I was telling him that I believed God brought us here together on this trip for a purpose. I wasn't sure why, but I felt it strongly none-the-less.

He told me that while he believed in God he found religion itself, as well as Pastor Kim's style, uncomfortable. I tried to convey to him that I knew God had been moving powerfully in my life this week, yet I was struggling to put it into words. So much had happened so quickly that I was still processing all that had occurred, and found it difficult to express. He listened intently, and I suddenly realized that his gaze was focused entirely on my face as I tried to articulate my thoughts and beliefs.

A surreal experience then occurred. I stopped talking; and met and held his gaze. Neither of us looked away, and in that moment time stood still as something wonderful happened to me. I have heard it said that the eyes are the windows to the soul. In that instant I felt our souls connect in a swirling spiritual way. I allowed this man all the way into my heart and soul. I trusted him completely and felt no need to put up walls to protect myself from him. The essence of who I was flowed freely with Jeff and it felt powerfully and emotionally intimate. The room faded away from my awareness as I focused completely on this sensation of complete trust and vulnerability.

I have no idea how long or short we held this pivotal gaze. It felt like it lasted a long time, yet it was probably only several moments. Like a bubble bursting, the spell was broken when the lights were raised and the barkeep announced it was closing time. We broke our gaze and I shook my head slightly. I felt disoriented as I gazed around the room taking in the late night city scene. The magical interlude had ended, but the emotions lingered and my heart felt strangely full. Leaving the bar, Jeff escorted me across the street to our hotel. We both laughed when we realized how we had lost track of time; it was 1:00 AM and we each had to be up in four hours to begin our trek to Zurich airport.

We exited the hotel elevator and stood in the hallway for a few minutes before going our separate ways. As we faced each other I smiled and playfully asked, "Three kisses?" remembering the cheek kisses he had given me on my birthday earlier in the week. He gave me a quick and unexpected goodnight kiss on the lips, which both startled me and warmed my heart at the same time. I went to my room and fell into bed happily exhausted knowing something significant had changed for me this night.

The alarm went off a few hours later and I sleepily arose and dressed for a day of air travel. Part of me was looking forward to going home and another part was reluctant to end my journey with this special group. I was especially dreading saying goodbye to Jeff. We boarded the bus for the Zurich airport amid the excited chatter of our tour group. There was an air of anticipation about returning home, as some of us fretted about the extra weight our souvenir purchases had added to our luggage.

When we arrived at the airport we bid Werner many thankful goodbyes as he dropped us at the terminal. Jeff escorted us inside and our group followed him like a large amoeba through the corridors to the check-in area. As had so often occurred in the past week, he and I fell into step alongside one another. I was never sure which of us initiated this now familiar synchronization, but we seemed to once again gravitate towards each other as the group walked and talked. I asked him when we would be parting ways so that I could say goodbye to him and he said it would be shortly. I suddenly felt a hard knot of dread in my stomach.

Our group joined the line of people in queue to check-in with the airline. Jeff informed us it would take about a half an hour to get through the check-in process. Our group quietly talked with one another, some continuing to worry about the weight limit of their luggage and making plans to pull and rearrange items if necessary. I saw Jeff working his way down the line saying goodbye to every person in the tour group. Some shook his hand and some gave him grateful hugs. I suddenly realized that this was it, and swallowed hard as he approached our little troupe.

Bobby, Mom, Annemarie, and Linda all gave him warm hugs. Then it was my turn. I gave him a smile of sincere affection, hugging him hard and swallowing around the lump in my throat. He looked me in the eye and we wished each other well, saying we would stay in touch. I was acutely aware that others were watching us; many in our group had witnessed the growing affection between us as the trip progressed, and they were curious to see how our parting would go. Their watchful attention made the moment all the more difficult. Others in the group were waiting to say goodbye to him so Jeff continued up the line. After the last person, he waved goodbye and we collectively waved back to him…and he left us.

I struggled with my emotions as I awaited my turn to check-in. Aware of my distress, Mom attempted to distract me with idle conversation. Soon I approached the counter and completed the necessary steps to board the trans-Atlantic flight. When finished, I stepped to the side and waited for the rest of my fellow travelers to join me. I stood there gazing absent-mindedly up at the departure and arrival board. I tried to focus through misty eyes at flight information for Paris, Peru, and London, while my heart tried not to break open. I realized with horror that I was going to lose it right here in this very public place. My throat was tight with the lump that was forming, and my eyes were in danger of overflowing at any minute. I didn't want to say goodbye to Jeff. I didn't know how or when it had happened this week, but I suddenly realized I had fallen in love with the tour guide. I felt like a character in a heart-breaking movie and thought, *This can't be happening to me.* I like having composure and being in control of my emotions, especially in public places.

As I stood there feeling the complete and total impact of my emotions, I was joined by my mother, Linda, and Bobby. I told them I was struggling to keep it together when suddenly Jeff appeared again. He came back pushing an airport luggage cart carrying his duffel bag and a wearing a huge grin on his face. "Hallo!" he greeted us as several exclaimed surprise at seeing him again. "Right then, I got my train ticket and have some time to kill before it leaves so I thought I would see you onto the next leg of your trip," he said with a smile.

He caught my eye and sent me a brilliant smile as I shakily smiled back. As emotional as I was feeling, I didn't trust myself to speak. He led our group up a ramp to the security line, and I quickly pulled myself together. I realized that this was an opportunity for me to say goodbye to him again, this time without a crowd around us. Calculating how long it would take us to get through airport procedures in order to board our flight, I estimated that I had about 30 minutes of time to spare.

Making a quick decision, I asked Linda if she would be willing to escort Mom, Annemarie, and Bobby through security and to the gate while I had a cup of coffee with Jeff. She looked compassionately at my emotion-filled faced and agreed saying, "Okay, but don't be too long. We don't want you to miss this flight." I reassured her that I wouldn't, and headed towards Jeff to invite him for a cup of coffee. He happily agreed and we walked to a nearby coffee stand, purchased our drinks, and stood at a bar-height table to sip them.

We chatted comfortably, and soon he fished a map out from his bag to show me the path his train would take on the way back to Munich. We also traced the route we had taken in Switzerland, and I explained where Maryland was located in the U.S. For the moment, we were distracted by the visual display of the geography that would separate us; only delaying the inevitable final goodbye.

We agreed again to stay in touch via Facebook, and he promised to set up Skype so that we could communicate that way as well. I was blindsided by the sudden intensity of my emotions now that we were departing, and knew I didn't want to let go of my connection with him. I had no idea *what* I was feeling. I just knew it was powerfully strong and special. We finished our drinks and he walked me back to the security line. Giving me a quick kiss on the cheek he said goodbye and was gone.

Feeling better about our parting I turned and went through security and was faced with a long, cavernous hallway to traverse. Rushing down the wide corridor to the gate, I glanced at my watch and realized I had pushed my time to the limit to savor my last few moments with Jeff. I arrived at the gate just as our plane was boarding. Linda and Mom hurried towards me with anxious faces, conveying their concern. Linda said, "Your mom was so worried you would miss the plane. I told her I would stay behind with you but I am *really* glad you are here!" With a big sigh of relief we all boarded the plane together.

As we settled into our seats for the long flight home, I felt much better having said goodbye to Jeff privately. I was grateful that he had returned and spent those last few minutes with me. I needed that and appreciated his thoughtfulness in showing up. I wasn't sure he fully realized the extent of the impact he'd had on me. It would take me months afterwards to decipher the events of these past two weeks.

I relaxed into my seat with a satisfied sigh. I was so glad I had come on this journey and been open to receive all the blessings God had offered me. Jeff and I had promised to stay in touch and I had high hopes that we would fulfill those intentions with one another. I reflected on the rainbow that God had provided the night before and I knew He would be with me no matter what. His promise was one I could count on forever, even in the midst of my roiling emotions and very human insecurities. The entire trip had been a mountaintop experience and I longed to stay in it, yet the journey had come to an end. My heart overflowed with new, intense feelings and I would need time to process them fully.

CHAPTER TWENTY
REFLECTION QUESTIONS

Discovering Soulful Connections

1. 'The eyes are the window to the soul.' What does this statement mean to you?

2. What has been your experience with deep and soulful looks?

3. When have you been surprised by the intensity of your feelings for someone else?

4. What did you learn from it?

PART 3
Found

The Treasure

I returned from Germany on cloud nine, convinced that I had fallen in love with Jeff. I certainly was displaying all of the signs. My days and nights were filled with longing for him as I replayed special moments from the trip over and over in my mind; all the while savoring the new emotions I felt in my heart. I had trouble focusing on my work, and chose instead to write lengthy e-mails to Jeff, in which I shared the details of my life. I wanted desperately to continue what we had started. Distracted by these feelings, I scanned my email frequently searching for his replies. They appeared regularly, although his responses were brief in contrast to my lengthy epistles.

I was a bit put-off by the shortness of his messages, but he explained that he was having some challenges with technology and encouraged me to keep writing. I felt like a school-girl again; carefree, giggling-happy, and somewhat flighty. This unfamiliar emotional state caught me off-guard. I felt as if I had left a piece of myself in Germany with Jeff.

Over the next few weeks I kept my flame burning for him; hoping we could eventually connect on Skype when he overcame his computer difficulties. Even though I knew he was sorting out his ambivalent feelings for someone else, I still held out hope for an ongoing relationship with him. I romantically fantasized about us traveling between continents to see one another. It was so unlike me to be acting this foolishly, and I was astonished at my own infatuated state. My heart was wide open and reeling with the intensity of these overpowering emotions. I felt unstable and found it difficult to get my bearings in those initial weeks after returning from the trip.

Realizing that there was a great deal to process about my experiences in Europe, and recognizing that Jeff was only one part of the story, I requested a meeting with my pastor, Susan. While having coffee and pastry in her office one day, I openly conveyed the unexpected joy and love I felt traveling with my mother, the flirtation with Jeff that turned into something deeper and more meaningful as I said goodbye, the healing God gave me at the Church in the Meadow, and my chance encounter with Greg. She listened intently as I spilled my complex story. While much of the account intrigued her, she was quick to observe that running into Greg while standing in a crowd of 4,700 people outside the theater in Oberammergau, Germany was no mere coincidence. We both wholeheartedly agreed that such moments of synchronicity were divine appointments orchestrated by the Holy Spirit. We also concurred that whenever one of these God-arranged moments occurs, it is wise to reflectively pause and ask ourselves, *Why did this happen and what does God want me to learn from it?* I had been asking myself that very question since returning home and it was now helpful to reflect aloud about it with my trusted spiritual advisor.

Susan enjoyed my entire story and counseled me to remain open to the lessons that God was showing me during this time. At one point in the conversation, she asked if I wanted to drop everything in my life and go live in Germany with Jeff, and I surprised myself by actually considering it. My mind said "no" but the longing in my heart said "yes"! Knowing how much I loved my life here, the awareness that I would even contemplate leaving it all for Jeff helped me to realize just how unsettling the powerful experiences from this trip were. I had to stop and ask myself at that moment, *Would I really leave behind my sons, my home, my work, and everything that I held dear to chase after these intense feelings?* I recognized that I was, quite frankly, in an emotional tailspin.

In addition to Susan, I thanked God for Linda. Like a true friend, she rode the waves of my emotions with me. Our post-trip conversations helped me to process all that had shifted in my life in such a short time. Her gentle observations, insights, and ability to connect the dots of what had occurred proved to be extremely valuable as I tried to comprehend the changes occurring within me.

A few weeks after our return home, Linda and I had dinner with Pastor Kim. She, too, had witnessed the budding romance between Jeff and me during the trip, and her confirmation validated my feelings and reassured me that I had not imagined it all. She reminded me that she had a dream about me on the first day of the trip and this had occurred prior to really knowing any of us, and certainly before anything started to develop between Jeff and me. She was now eager to share the rest of the dream with us over dinner.

Kim began by repeating what she had previously told us in Oberammergau. While resting on her bed that first day in Germany, she had drifted into a half awake state and dreamed that I had a baby girl that I was carrying around and showing to everyone. I was overflowing with joy about my baby and enthusiastically introducing her to our tour group. What Kim hadn't told me the first time was that Jeff was also in the dream. But now she shared the rest of the story. "Jeff was there, too. You and he were in love. He didn't speak, but was quietly watching you show your baby to

THE TREASURE

everyone." I received this surprising information and pondered the meaning of it. I felt sure that the baby in Kim's dream represented my own inner child. I thought again what a special woman Kim was as I realized she intuitively saw the unfolding vision of love in my life before it had even happened. Now with hindsight, I was able to appreciate the full meaning of Kim's perceptive dream that day. I cherished our shared realization that Jeff had played a part in my awakening heart.

Kim was quick to caution me, however, not to be so anxious to give my heart away to Jeff. Despite the obvious attraction between the two of us, she warned me not to chase after him and to hold back a bit. She said almost prophetically, "Carol, you are a treasure, and you don't need to convince a man to cherish you. Someone will come along who will truly recognize the treasure that you are and he will seek you. Wait for it." She then went on to say, "Men are hardwired to be hunters and to search for their prize. Let yourself be found by the man who is looking for you. While it is clear God put Jeff in your life for a reason, just recognize that he might not be *the* one."

As I listened to Kim's advice, I was struck yet again by the depth of wisdom in this young pastor. Even though I loved hearing that I was a treasure, I couldn't stop myself from chasing after the intensely happy feelings I had in Germany. I longed for the joyful excitement I had experienced there and was determined not to let go of those feelings.

After our dinner that night, I continued to write to Jeff often. However, taking Kim's advice into consideration, I shortened the length of the e-mails and tried to channel the floodwaters of my emotions. This heady feeling of being in love was both confusing and stimulating. I was struggling to focus on my work and life. I still found myself daydreaming of my time with Jeff and considering the possibility of a future together.

As the days passed, I attempted to make sense of it all. I asked myself, *What was the magic I felt on the trip?* The answer was that I was joyful, open, trusting, and free. I was completely comfortable with who I was, and felt confident in sharing my authentic self with others. I had also experienced a deep and unconditional love with my Mom. She is the one who had known me from the moment my life began, and this love was powerful in and of itself. Building upon that trusting relationship, I was finally learning to accept and love myself as the unique individual God created me to be. I began to understand that this was the true gift of the healing, and deep inside I pondered that awareness. Could it be that the real love story here was not my relationship with Jeff, but with God?

The magnitude of these thoughts overwhelmed me and as I struggled to fully grasp them, I retreated to my familiar pattern of focusing on others. It was much easier to concentrate on Jeff and fan the fire of my feelings for him than to realize that he may have just been a transient person in my life.

A month after our return from abroad Jeff wrote me an e-mail saying that his relationship life was a mess. He began by saying that he never committed to the relationship with the woman in India. This didn't surprise me, and in some strange way, it validated that there was indeed something between

> Could it be that the real love story was...with God?

us. The rest of his email, however, shocked me as he explained that he had just begun a new relationship with a woman twenty years younger than himself. He was writing freely to me of his concerns and struggles with both women, and asked for my advice and counsel.

Absorbing this news, I felt as if I had been punched in the stomach. I was hurt, deflated, and disappointed. I have to admit, though, that I was also a bit relieved. This entire experience with him had taken me well out of my comfort zone. Hearing that he was moving on to a new relationship was painful, yet it also released me from my farfetched daydreams of international romance, which would risk upsetting my entire world.

I was pleased that he felt comfortable enough to share his struggles with me. Unfortunately, his honesty forced me to admit that our connection in Germany did not hold the same intensity for him as it did for me. He clearly saw me more as a friend than a love interest.

I soon settled into the safe boundaries of friend and advisor to Jeff and our correspondence became less frequent. I held onto a feeble hope that he would eventually return my feelings of affection, but I realized that it might take a long time if it ever happened at all. Seeking normalcy, I resumed the tried-and-true habits that had always given purpose to my life. I busied myself with work, family, and friends as the excitement and thrill of my international experiences started to fade.

**CHAPTER TWENTY-ONE
REFLECTION QUESTIONS**
Discovering Your Treasure

1. When have you experienced the freedom to be open, trusting, and fully yourself?

2. In what ways are you learning to love and accept yourself as the unique individual that God created you to be?

3. What challenges you to truly believe that you are a treasure?

4. What is the love story between you and God?

CHAPTER 22

Greg

As my emotions about Jeff started to settle, I began to pay attention to a quiet inner question that had arisen in my mind since I had returned home. *Why had God arranged for Greg and me to run into each other in Germany?* I eventually decided to satisfy my curiosity and acted on a persistent nudge to reach out to him. I emailed and suggested that we get together to talk about our respective trips abroad. He immediately agreed and we met for dinner on an outdoor patio at a local brewery in late August. It was a warm summer evening and it pleasantly reminded me of dining at an outdoor café in Europe.

In his mid-fifties, Greg was slightly taller than me, with kind blue eyes and a friendly smile beneath his bushy mustache. He was a nice looking man with a closely-cropped but full head of hair sprinkled with gray, which made him look distinguished. He was neatly dressed in khakis and a sports shirt, and I appreciated the care he took with his appearance. I anticipated getting to know this soft-spoken and gentle man as he pulled out my chair for me to be seated.

Our conversation flowed comfortably as we ordered drinks and discussed the various beers we had each tasted in Germany. Soon we were sharing stories from some our favorite parts of the trip, our impressions of the Passion Play, and laughing over funny anecdotes with one another.

Although Greg and I were acquaintances from years ago when both our families had attended the same church, I had never spent time with just him and wasn't quite sure what to expect. He was both familiar to me and at the same time, was like a stranger. I was happy to learn that he had a calm way about him, was a good listener, and that we shared a similar sense of humor. He seemed comfortable in his own skin; a trait that I have noticed has a way of putting others at ease as well.

After our dinner, we parted ways and I went home with my heart warmed by our time together. A part of me was still missing Germany and my experiences there, but I was glad I had reached out to Greg. He and I shared the same perspective that God had put us in each other's paths for a reason; even though we didn't know yet what that reason might be.

A few days later, Greg contacted me and said that he had enjoyed our evening together so much that he would like to take me to a German restaurant for dinner. I accepted his invitation to drive to a nearby town to experience authentic Alpine cuisine. Oompah music was playing as we dined on traditional German dishes of sauerkraut and Wiener Schnitzel. Although it was a pleasant experience, I found it difficult to enjoy myself completely. Being surrounded by an abundance of German memorabilia, music, and food was a poignant reminder of Jeff and I ended up spending much of the evening feeling distracted and uneasy.

I thanked Greg for the dinner, not really expecting to hear from him again. My initial curiosity had been met and aside from friendship, I had no expectations of anything further between us. I was still carrying a torch for Jeff and Greg was clearly still grieving the loss of his wife. Within a week, though, Greg did contact me about getting together again. This time I suggested we do something active instead of going out to dinner and we agreed to spend the evening walking around the Frederick County Fair. I said I would meet him there but he said, "No, I will pick you up. Call me old-fashioned, but I believe a man should pick up a woman to take her out." I was both surprised by his philosophy and charmed at the same time. What surprised me even more was my own reaction of acceptance. In the past, the independent woman in me would have pushed back to claim autonomy. But now I was more than happy to be taken care of, which felt different and unfamiliar.

We walked around the fairgrounds, eating food from concessionaires and looking at the animals, while country music drifted over the crowds. The sweet smell of cotton candy mingled with the earthy smell of animals and created an olfactory smorgasbord. We wandered along with the crowd; taking in the sights of huge tractors, hot tub displays, and the giant Ferris wheel that loomed over the distant midway. It was an enjoyable evening as we immersed ourselves in the agricultural atmosphere. There were times when Greg reached out a hand to guide me and I wondered if he wanted to hold my hand, but he never did, so I thought, *Perhaps he is just being gentlemanly.*

Afterwards, we returned to my house to sit on the deck and enjoy the warm summer evening under the glow of a full moon. Greg was quiet and I felt that I was carrying the conversation. I knew that he hadn't dated since his wife, Lori, died in a car accident just 21 months earlier, so I was sensitive to how difficult this must have been for him. He shared with me that he and Lori had been high school sweethearts, so he hadn't dated anyone but her for his entire life. I knew how much he had loved her and could only guess at what he had been through since losing her so suddenly. I was in unfamiliar territory, so I filled the space with my own chatty conversation; hoping that it would somehow make us both feel more comfortable. Our fun evening started to become draining as I struggled to keep the conversation going. I had never spent so much time with such a quiet man before and I was uneasy with the awkward lulls in the conversation.

The next day, Greg sent me flowers with a card that said, "Just because you are who you are." I saved it, knowing that there was something very special about this man who could see and accept me for who I was. I reflected how in past relationships when I was with a man, I tended to adapt or change my behavior to accommodate his needs (or more accurately what I perceived he wanted and needed). This made it difficult for any man to be truly close to me since I was an enigma. I wasn't clear about who I was and constantly shifted to be what I thought someone else wanted me to be. Influenced by my past experiences with my dad and ex-husband, I did a dance of anxious attachment in my relationships that had never worked.

I continued to reflect on the fact that I hadn't done that dance with Jeff, nor was I doing it with Greg. Perhaps having finally learned to love and accept myself, I was feeling more confident just being me. The thought occurred to me that this might be due to the fact that the relationships with both Jeff and Greg were platonic. Whatever the reasons, there were

> Perhaps having finally learned to love and accept myself, I was feeling more confident just being me.

no pretenses between Greg and me. We were enjoying an open, honest, and slow-growing friendship.

Later that fall when Greg asked me to join him and three other couples for dinner, I hesitated, knowing that these couples had been very close friends with him and Lori. I felt as if there were some really big shoes to fill if I were to be at Greg's side during this dinner. I pondered what to do or say. Eventually, I decided to address my concerns openly with him. He reassured me that his friends would accept me, but I was still uncertain. I said, "I'm not really sure what we're doing together and I don't want to give the impression that we're a couple when we're not. I just know God put us in each other's lives for a reason so we're hanging out together. I think I may just be here to help you with your healing and transition through grief."

I think he treasures me.

Greg commented, "Maybe we're each here to help the other with a transition." This honest conversation was deeper and more vulnerable than any other we had exchanged thus far. The truth of his statement landed with a soft thud on my heart, causing me to emit a low *huh* at this insight. His frank observation about the mutual benefit of us spending time together opened my eyes to see that it wasn't just about me helping him through a hard time. He was right; I was benefitting from our friendship as well.

He was clearly moving through the changing stages of grief. Less obvious were the many lessons I was learning about myself and my relationships with men. Barely understanding them myself, I was unable to explain them to Greg. With this one statement, however, he showed me that he intuitively knew he was in my life to help with that growth. We were travel partners on this part of life's journey and we were both trying to trust what was unfolding between us.

Our discussion showed me the depth of Greg's emotional intelligence and I developed a new appreciation for this wise, gentle man. As a result of our discussion, I decided to accept the dinner invitation and was warmly welcomed by his friends. They recognized the challenges of the situation and went to great lengths to put me at ease.

Afterwards, I continued to acknowledge the new and unfamiliar feelings I was having as I sought to accept what was an entirely new kind of relationship; unlike any I had ever experienced before.

In the early winter months, a friend asked me how things were going with Greg and I said, "There's something really different about him. When I was sick he showed up with soup and visited with me in my less-than-attractive condition. When it snowed he showed up with a snow blower to clear my driveway and then he went on his way. He gives to me without expecting anything in return. He shows up. He's thoughtful and not self-centered. I think he *treasures* me." Finally, I was beginning to understand what Pastor Kim was trying to tell me months earlier.

By mid-winter I was truly wondering where things were going with Greg and me. It certainly seemed like a dating relationship, yet he hadn't even held my hand, much less kissed me. By his own admission, he was old-fashioned and knew how to behave like a gentleman. I had never spent so much time dating a man platonically and was quite unaccustomed to his reserved behavior. I was baffled by our six-month apparent dating relationship and began to question if he even had a romantic interest in me. Our growing friendship was pleasant yet I wondered if he would be hurt or disappointed if I decided to move on. He had been through so much already and I knew that I didn't want to be the cause of anymore heartache in his life.

Those speculations ended one February night after a lovely dinner, when we finally kissed and ignited the passion between us that had lain dormant thus far. My worries were relieved as I realized that indeed there was a romantic interest between us, and our friendship evolved to a deeper level of intimacy.

I later asked Greg what he was going through during those six months that we were spending time together as just friends and he said, "Carol, I was in a desert. I told myself, and everyone else, that I was okay but I wasn't. During that first year after Lori died, I was focused on our daughter, Karen, and being there for her. As time went on, and she was doing better, friends and family expressed their worry about me. I would tell them that I was fine, to alleviate their concerns. But the truth is that I was wandering in a desert of grief." As I listened to his honest and heart-wrenching revelation, I was struck silent. His words touched my heart and I began to understand why he had been so quiet when we were together in the fall. He was slowly finding his way out of an emotional wilderness.

CHAPTER TWENTY-TWO
REFLECTION QUESTIONS
Discovering Your Way

1. What experiences in your life have caused you to feel as if you were lost in an emotional wilderness?

2. What has helped, or is helping, you to find your way out?

3. What individuals or groups did the universe put in your life to guide you?

4. What would it be like to believe that the people in your life right now are there for a reason?

5. What helps you to see challenges as opportunities for growth?

6. What would it feel like to receive each day as a gift from God signed 'just because you are who you are'?

CHAPTER *23*

Falling in Love (Again)

"Do you believe in signs?" Greg asked me one day. "I do," was my reply, and then asked "Why?" He went on to tell me that sometime after Lori's memorial service he had thoroughly gone through her wallet. A business card with a compelling name, *Life Wellspring,* caught his eye and he recognized my picture on it. He wasn't sure why Lori had my business card but, not yet ready to get rid of her belongings, he decided to hold onto it.

Greg's discovery surprised me and instantly brought to mind the last time I had seen Lori. I had run into her at a networking event just two weeks prior to the accident. We had spoken and exchanged business cards. Prior to that, it had been ten years since we had last seen each other. We were both surprised and glad to reconnect.

Lori had always been a very talkative woman and she spent most of our 20-minute conversation telling me about her daughter Karen's wedding, which had taken place four months earlier. Lori was not only delighted with Karen's new husband but also with her choice of a career in music therapy and hospice care. She glowed with animation and pride as she told me about the details of her only child's life. As she spoke I could imagine the transformation of Karen from a redheaded, outgoing, young girl into the lovely young woman her mother was now describing.

Lori then shifted the conversation and asked about my sons and my work. I updated her on my children and described my recent training as a coach. Since she worked in human resources, Lori was interested in my choice of a second career and asked for my business card. We hugged goodbye and she had apparently put my card in her wallet.

Greg appreciated hearing the story of how my card had come to be in her possession. Together we pondered this apparent sign of God connecting us with one another before we were even aware of it. He then went onto tell me about another sign. When Lori had died, he and Karen had received overwhelming support from family, friends, their church, and the entire community. Lori was well known and respected in our area and there was an outpouring of grief when she, along with others, died in a multiple car pile-up on an interstate highway on a snowy January day.

In addition to a steady stream of people offering help, Greg and Karen had received hundreds of cards of sympathy and concern. Cherishing the sentiments they expressed, Karen eventually tied them with ribbons into bundles and stored them in shoe boxes. Greg explained that he had gone to the closet recently and had randomly opened one of the boxes to read some of the cards again. "Of all the boxes and all the cards, do you know which card I pulled out first?" he asked.

I shook my head as I listened intently. "The first one I picked up was from you. Do you know what it said?" he asked.

My eyes widened with surprise and I again shook my head, not remembering what I had written more than two years earlier. Greg said, "You had written in the card to Karen and me that you were so sorry for our loss. You wrote that you were praying that God would provide us with just what we needed." Facing me and looking right in my eyes he asked, "Did you know it would be you?" His question landed with a soft thud on my chest as I absorbed the impact of his words and the meaning of both of these signs.

We pondered together how God had been moving unbeknownst to us, providing such simple, yet meaningful, markers. We were in awe of these personal examples of prevenient grace; the kind of grace in which God mercifully provides what we require before we are even aware of our need for help.

Greg and I continued to date regularly and grew closer as a couple. In March, he said that he would like to re-introduce me to his daughter, Karen, and her husband, Justin. I hadn't seen Karen since she was about 12 years old, with the exception of a brief sympathetic exchange at her mother's memorial service. I was looking forward to meeting this special young woman who clearly was the apple of her father's eye. Karen was pregnant with twins that were due in early May, so we decided to get together soon, knowing how limited their time would be after the babies arrived. We made a plan for the four of us to have dinner when I returned from an upcoming writing weekend. As so often happens, things did not go exactly as we had planned.

While on my writing retreat, Greg texted to advise me that Karen had been admitted to the hospital for high blood pressure. She had been very healthy throughout her pregnancy but now, in a matter of days, the situation had changed dramatically. She was told to stop working and to immediately go on bed rest. Greg apologized for interrupting my writing, but I assured him that I wanted to hear from him. I felt concerned for Karen's well-being and I wanted to be supportive of Greg. I compassionately understood his fatherly apprehension for the health of his only child and soon-to-be grandbabies. As we exchanged text messages and calls over the course of a day I experienced a dawning realization of how deeply I had come to care for this gentle man; much more than I had previously realized. It was in this crisis that I recognized that I wanted to be the person he turned to with his concerns and his joys. I began to realize that he had gradually moved into my inner circle and taken up residence in my heart. Our slowly evolving relationship had become deep and meaningful and this time of distress illuminated that clearly to me.

I didn't get much writing done that weekend but I gained an important insight about the two of us. When I returned we adjusted our plans to accommodate the new situation. Instead of going out to dinner, Greg and I went to the hospital to meet Karen and Justin. Fortunately, Karen was feeling well and was in good spirits. This certainly wasn't where we had imagined we would meet but it was comfortable and friendly nonetheless. We had plenty to talk about with the babies on the way. Greg and I actually spent more time conversing with Justin than with Karen as we walked to the cafeteria to eat with him while Karen rested. The doctors had told them that a Caesarean section would be performed in one week if her blood pressure remained stable.

Greg visited Karen at the hospital daily and I could see his fatherly devotion. He told me that he and Karen had always had a close relationship but it had become even closer since her mom had died. He talked to Karen on the phone every day even before she was in the hospital.

Karen remained stable that week and the C-section was scheduled for the following Monday. I told Greg that I would be available to support him in any way that he needed on the day Karen had her surgery. He appreciated my offer but was unsure of what he wanted or needed. A few days later I received a text from Karen asking me if I would like to be present on the day of the twins' births. I was so touched by her message that I immediately called her and said, "Thank you for thinking of me and asking me to be there. I recognize what a momentous day in your life this will be and I would love to be a part of it, but only if you and your dad are comfortable with me being there."

Karen replied, "Carol, I appreciate you saying that. I know it is really important to my dad that you are there and I am fine with it, too. I hope you will plan to be with us." I was impressed by Karen's gracious maturity and her sincere love for her father. I told her I would be delighted to be present.

The day that Karen and Justin were to become parents dawned with a pink sky as Greg and his good friend, Paula, picked me up to travel eastward to the hospital. Paula and her husband, Bob, were Greg's best friends and they planned to spend the day at the hospital with us. They were like a special aunt and uncle to Karen and wouldn't have missed the birth of these babies for the world. Bob was meeting us there later in the day. Paula and I chatted excitedly while Greg drove the one hour to the hospital. He was pensive and preoccupied with his thoughts, clearly anxious to get there.

When we arrived at the hospital we were told that we couldn't go up to visit Karen because she already had six visitors in her room. She was in a special unit for preeclampsia patients and there was a limit to the number of visitors she could have at one time. Both sets of parents from Justin's blended family were present, as well as Greg, Paula, Bob, and me. Greg was clearly stressed that he couldn't go upstairs immediately, but we graciously went to the family waiting room to sit and chat with Justin's mother and stepfather.

Soon Greg received a call from Karen that she wanted him, and he grabbed my hand and started to walk purposefully towards the elevators. Chris, Justin's mom, said, "Paula, what about you? You should go." I looked at Paula and felt torn as I knew how close she was to Karen. They had been through so much together. Like Chris, I thought Paula should go too, but Greg wanted me by his side so I gave a backward glance of apology to Paula over my shoulder as we left the waiting area.

When we arrived in Karen's room she looked lovely and there was a definite glow about her. One of the benefits of a C-section is the orderly and planned manner of the birth. Both of my babies were born at unexpected times, so I was impressed by the calm and organized atmosphere of this morning. Karen was wearing a pretty lavender robe and had even put on a little makeup. She clearly had taken time to pamper herself a bit and I was happy to see this. After all, it was a big day for her. She waddled around the room with a hand on her huge belly while Justin checked his phone for messages.

Greg walked over and gave her a kiss and she relayed all that had transpired since the last time they had spoken. There was an air of excitement and anticipation permeating the room as we talked quietly. After spending a few minutes with Greg, Karen, and Justin, I was conscious of ending my visit so that Paula could come up to see Karen before she went into surgery.

Karen had been pacing restlessly and fidgeted with the blankets trying to settle herself onto her bed. As I prepared to leave I wondered what I could do to reassure her. Trusting an inner nudge, I asked, "Have you prayed yet today?"

She seemed taken aback by the question and thought about it a moment. In a surprised tone she answered "Why, no, I haven't."

Not wanting to be presumptuous I asked, "Would you like to?"

Her immediate reply was "Yes!" Karen settled herself on the bed and everyone gathered around and held hands. We were bowing our heads when the door burst open and Karen's energetic Aunt Suzanne (Lori's sister) entered with two of her daughters. Suzanne and her daughters had somehow gotten past the nurses who were limiting the number of visitors Karen could have at one time. Karen welcomed them by saying, "Oh good, you're just in time. We're getting ready to pray." They quickly joined us in the prayer circle around Karen's hospital bed and we bowed our heads together again.

I looked up at Greg and asked, "Do you want to say the prayer?" and he replied, "No, you can do it."

I bowed my head again, and opening my heart to the Holy Spirit, I began to pray out loud. I prayed for protection over Karen that day and for the doctors and nurses to take great care of her and the two babies about to be born. I prayed for the skill and expertise of the medical staff. Lastly, I prayed about Lori. "Dear Lord, we know you are right here in this room with us and that Lori's spirit is here with us as well. Help us to feel Yours and her presence, and to know that we are loved and cared for. Bless Karen with the presence of her Mom as she becomes a mother herself this day. Amen."

As I ended the prayer my heart was full of love and the peaceful assurance that only comes from God. Wiping tears from her eyes, Karen thanked me and peacefully said she was ready now. I kissed her forehead and left to get Paula, while Greg remained there with her until it was time to prep her for the C-section.

Later, as I sat quietly knitting beside Greg in the waiting area, he received a picture text message from Justin of his first grandson, Parker Gregory. He passed the phone around so that everyone could see it and many in the room burst into spontaneous tears. Relief and joy mixed with sorrow over the fact that Lori wasn't physically there to share in the experience with them. I gently rubbed Greg's back until his emotions subsided, and then a second picture was sent, this time of Jacob Preston. Two healthy baby boys were now in the world! What a blessing they would be to this family.

I was honored to be a part of such a transformational day. When Greg went upstairs to see Karen and Justin and to hold his grandsons for the first time, his best friend Bob came and sat beside me. A novice knitter, I was attempting baby hats for the boys. I carefully put my needles down and glanced at Bob questioningly. He is typically a joyful soul and usually was a kidder whenever we interacted so I was surprised that he was now completely serious. Looking directly into my eyes he said with heartfelt honesty, "I am *so* glad you are here. It means the world to us that you are."

I responded with equal sincerity "I wouldn't want to be anywhere else, Bob." The truth of that statement resonated in my heart and must have been apparent on my face. I continued, "This is all about Greg for me."

Understanding that I was entirely present to support his friend, he gratefully replied, "It warms my heart to see my buddy happy again and it's because of you." My eyes misted over to hear his straightforward affirmation welcoming my presence in Greg's life, and on this special occasion. It confirmed what I already knew in my own heart; I was right where I belonged.

When I got the chance to hold the babies later that day I gazed into the depths of their eyes and felt a deep connection with their newborn souls. They had just come from God. I was surprised again by the intensity of the feelings that are possible in long, loving looks when souls swirl together. Gazing into their eyes I pondered the mystery of what it's like to travel from the other side of the veil to here. These were indescribably beautiful moments. I quietly savored how precious they were, thinking to myself how fortunate I was to be part of their first hours of life.

Later that day, Suzanne pulled me aside and echoed Bob's sentiments. "Thank you for being here, she said. It means so much to everyone that you are with us." I was surprised because she was Lori's sister and I thought she might have found it awkward having me present on this special day for their family. She continued, "You are not only good for Greg, but for Karen and the rest of us, too. Thank you so much." Her acceptance and grace filled my being with a warm glow as I smiled and hugged her.

When we left that night and headed home our hearts were full of love and relief that all had gone smoothly. Both mother and babies were doing well and we could rest easily after all the worry we had been feeling leading up to this day. Even though it was late when Greg and I arrived back at my house, we sat on the couch and quietly talked; continuing to process the details of the day. Greg eventually looked me in the eyes and said, "I want to tell you something and I don't want it to scare you."

With a slightly quivering voice I said, "Okay, what is it?" Seeing the serious look in his eyes I anticipated what was coming next.

He turned to face me, half kneeling, and said "I think I'm falling in love with you."

I took a shaky breath and as I exhaled I said, "I know… I'm falling in love with you, too." We smiled, kissed, and held each other tenderly, sharing the sweetness of the moment and recognizing that a longing in our hearts had been filled. We had been on a healing journey together for eight months. We had trusted our inner nudges to continue to move forward despite being unsure of where it was leading. Like coming out of a fog, we could now see the depths of our feelings for one another. Our faithfulness to follow the inner guidance God had provided along the way brought us to this moment of unmistakable conscious love.

CHAPTER TWENTY-THREE
REFLECTION QUESTIONS
Discovering Love and Grace

1. In what ways do you recognize and follow your inner nudges, especially as they pertain to relationships?

2. What has been your experience of awakening to conscious love?

3. The definition of prevenient grace is God providing what you need before you even know you need it; what has been your experience of such grace?

CHAPTER *24*

Lost and Found

I had found a treasure in Greg, and with this awareness our relationship deepened. Ultimately, I realized my longing for Jeff had been an infatuation. I had reconnected with my joyful spirit in Europe, and my immature self had fallen for the tour guide. Swept away by the flood of feelings unleashed by the healings of my heart, I misinterpreted that Jeff was the source of those emotions. As my walls came down, I found and reconnected with lost parts of my heart and soul. My lifelong search for wholeness of body, heart, mind, and spirit took a leap forward as I experienced increasing acceptance and unconditional love for myself. My feelings for Jeff were a necessary gateway on the pathway to romantic love again. I am forever grateful for my connection with him and the gift he unknowingly gave me by being a trustworthy and steady presence during a transformative time in my life.

My trek towards mature emotional love continued as I trusted God's plan for Greg and me. We had chosen to believe that God had crossed our paths for a reason, even if we didn't know what that reason was. We opted to be open to the possibilities that we felt God guiding us towards and relinquished control over the outcome. We trusted our intuition and faithfully acted on subtle nudges to spend time together and to grow in friendship. As our hearts individually healed, the gifts that we were to one another became clear. God, our matchmaker, had delighted and blessed us both with this unexpected relationship.

The greatest treasure, however, was the love that I found in my deepening relationship with God. This bond grew more meaningful as I learned to accept myself as a unique creation. Believing that I am valued and cherished by God was the most important lesson of all. Quenching my thirst for love from this unlimited divine source alleviated my need to look for it in others. It allowed me to discern the complexities of my relationships with more confidence. I learned to trust and believe that my connection with God would always ground and stabilize me as I faced the surprises and challenges of life.

I now view my relationship with Greg as a love triangle. God is at the apex and Greg and I are opposite one another at the base. As we each grow in our love for God, we travel up the sides of the triangle and draw closer to one another.

This triangular balance provides a flow of unconditional love that allows me to simultaneously achieve the intimacy and interdependence that I have always longed for. Within this framework, I am now free to love and be loved without losing myself or feeling the need to maintain emotional distance from others. I can create these triangles with everyone I love when I bring God into the relationship. Doing so permits me to completely be myself, while trusting that the other person is also on a journey towards spiritual awareness and fulfillment. The triangle provides boundaries that create a stable structure for healthy and balanced connections.

With this perspective, I now see that each relationship I have is a treasured love triangle which sparkles with its own unique beauty. When I put these many relationships together, I have a colorful kaleidoscope of love through which I can see and experience the heart connections that reflect God's presence in my life.

God, himself, is like an amazingly intricate kaleidoscope. In my humanness I have only been able to glimpse certain dimensions of His radiance at different times in my life. During times of crisis, significant shifts in my faith have occurred as I discovered new aspects of God's grace. Less dramatic shifts have occurred on a daily basis when I purposefully focus on developing my connection to God. The three centering beliefs I have introduced are the foundation for my approach to faith-based living. When I regularly apply these beliefs my eyes and heart are opened and I feel a personal connection with the Divine. Focusing daily on these beliefs creates an inner strength which I can depend upon when facing life's challenges.

The dictionary defines beliefs as a mental acceptance of our conviction in the truth or actuality of something. Faith, on the other hand, is believing in what we can't see, what is not tangible, and in some cases what does not even make sense at the moment. As we become more aware of our beliefs and adopt them as our own, they lead to further development of our personal faith.

I don't know what challenges you have been through in your life or what pain you have known, and I don't know where you find yourself now. I'd like to encourage you, however, to invite faith to be a part of your support system. I hope that you will continue to explore these three beliefs for faith-based living and discover what insights they hold for you.

Three Centering Beliefs for Faith-Based Living

God is personal and present.
God guides and provides.
God heals our hearts swiftly and silently.

I. God is personal and present

This belief maintains that there is a place within each of us that longs for a connection with something bigger than ourselves and that this longing can only be satisfied by a spiritual relationship with a Higher Being. There is a mystery to this Being which exists beyond the physical world and offers us an abundance of comfort, strength, and peace. As with any relationship, we need to spend time together in order to cultivate and deepen the bond. It is important that we each find our own meaningful connection to this Higher Being; perhaps through meditation, prayer, journaling, reading, singing, movement, or simply by being still. The details of where, when, and how we connect with God are unique to each of us. By exploring and developing our own spirituality, we discover the many ways in which love is magnified in our lives by this omnipresent Source.

My own faith journey has taken me along a winding path that has led to a surprising and abiding relationship with Jesus. After initially rejecting him, I now consider Him to be my teacher, guide, and best friend. He provides a bridge of understanding between my human experience and the Divine, which helps me to accept and love myself and others. In order to get to where I am today, I had to let go of my judgmental opinions and strive to maintain an open mind and heart as I sought to understand the many dimensions of God. In my faith journey, I explored various spiritual practices and holy sites, and gradually found what was meaningful to me. The experience was similar to putting together a puzzle; over time I found the pieces that I needed to make a personally significant connection with God. In hindsight, I see that God has always been there for me. What I didn't understand, however, was that before I could be fully present in my relationship with Him, I needed to know, love, and accept myself.

It is easy to get caught in the snare of self-judgment and criticism, thinking perfection is the goal. An inner critical voice whispers that I am not good enough, smart enough, attractive enough, or strong enough. Learning to override these insecurities and trust that God will help me wherever I fall short has allowed me to accept my imperfections more and more. His presence is a safety net that reassures me as I move through life. When I invite Him into the big and small details of daily life, I dance in partnership with God and allow Him to lead me from fear and doubt to hope and trust.

Self-care is an important aspect of my personal relationship with God. This self-care is not to be confused with self-centeredness or self-absorption. It means, instead, to be responsible for the care of my physical, emotional, mental, and spiritual well-being so that I can be fully present in all of my relationships. Taking time to re-fuel and nourish myself when I need food, rest, love, and laughter leads to a conscientious habit of being fully present in my own body, heart, and soul. When I practice this state of self-care and presence, I am able to show up and contribute to my own life and the lives of others in a balanced way.

Healthy boundaries are another benefit of my personal relationship with God. I spent much of my life without well-defined boundaries. There were times I focused on others to avoid my own emotional pain. The more self-aware and accepting I have become, the more I am able to acknowledge and accept others with deeper compassion and tolerance. By letting go of my need to control outcomes, I am better able to live interdependently with others. I no longer avoid discomfort by using the polar extremes of losing myself in caring for others, or maintaining an isolating self-protective distance. I am able to maintain a dynamic balance in the middle ground now.

Like the woman in the parable who lost her coin and searched every nook and cranny to find it, my personal journey towards a relationship with God was the lost coin I was seeking. And like that woman, I have celebrated and rejoiced with others when I found what was missing in my life.

Each of us is capable of having a deep and rewarding relationship with a Higher Being. I encourage you to seek it in your own way and to take the time to celebrate what you find along your lifelong faith journey.

II. God guides and provides

"You are a treasure. Let yourself be found." These were the words that Pastor Kim had said to me when I returned from Germany, and these words continue to guide my thoughts and actions today. Each of us is a one-of-a-kind gemstone that sparkles with multi-faceted radiance. When we polish our unique qualities, it allows us to radiate the love, passion, and joy that are our gifts to the world.

When we take care of ourselves in order to be the best we can be each day, we focus our attention on that which we can manage and take our focus off of people and circumstances over which we have no control. As much as we may want to, we cannot change others or many of the situations that occur in our lives. We can, however, choose to think, feel, and act in accordance with our own best self, and thus create an outward ripple of positive energy towards others.

Initially, the concept of self-care seemed counter-intuitive. I questioned how taking care of me would help others. It felt indulgent and I didn't see how it could provide balance and well-being in my life. I prided myself on being a problem solver and a planner; qualities that were helpful in creating accomplishments at work and at home. I had often barreled along in a headstrong fashion when I thought I knew the solution to a particular problem. As I learned to take small steps towards nurturing my own well-being, I began to realize the benefits of giving from a full and satisfied center instead of a needy and partially empty core.

With this belief I release my need for control and choose to trust God instead. Letting Him lead has been challenging. It requires that I balance my pragmatic skills with faith. Believing that God is continually guiding and providing requires that I give up my independent approach to life and embrace the perspective 'not my will but Yours be done.'

When I invited God to be my matchmaker, I chose to be open to His universal guidance and provision. As I let go of my plan and trusted that there was a divine plan, I began to notice an expanding strength in my soul. Learning to trust the guidance I receive from Him has been a process, especially when I don't fully understand the direction in which He is leading me. As I trust the guidance of the spirit within me I often say to God, *I don't know why You want me to do this, but I'm going to do it anyway, just because You nudged me.*

To be honest, I dance back and forth between taking and releasing control, but with each step I take towards letting go, the benefits increase. I experience peace and assurance as I replace my striving and worry with faith and trust.

I now invite God to guide me each day to the people, places, and experiences that He has designed for my benefit. Sometimes His nudges are obvious to me and other times they are so subtle that I almost miss them. As I use the first belief and cultivate a personal relationship with God, I am open to this second belief and am more likely to recognize His guidance and respond to what is being provided. By putting my trust and faith in this divine partnership, I receive direction for my daily activities. This illuminates and strengthens my inner glow and allows me to be of service to others without losing myself.

III. God heals our hearts swiftly and silently

Along my journey to find my own relationship with God, I experienced a progression of heart healings. When I released control and trusted in His divine plan for my life, I became a willing partner in my own growth. Instead of independently forcing my way, I learned to look for, and trust, God's guidance. Even when His way seemed unusual and surprising, I reminded myself to believe in it. I move forward tentatively at times, but proceed nonetheless because I trust that God has "plans to prosper me and not to harm me" *(Jeremiah 29:11)*. The heart healings I have received have led me to a deeper understanding of myself and God.

I believe God is a loving Being who is ever present with humanity; in both the good and bad times. As I turn towards God and maintain a personal relationship with Him, my heart and soul are restored. Transformational healing moments have occurred when I least expected them, often when I was at the end of my rope; too tired to try anymore. In these moments of exhaustion, I finally got out of my own way, accepted things as they were, and asked for help. In doing so I became willing to receive divine assistance.

Powerful healing moments have occurred swiftly and silently as I connected to, and received, the God-energy in and around me. These transformational healing moments have left me thinking, *I don't know what just happened, but I feel different inside.* I experienced an inner peaceful calm and felt in awe of the mysterious power that touched and changed my heart. In those moments I surrendered my will to God's will and trusted Him completely. Even though there have been markedly powerful moments that have reconciled and changed my heart, smaller healing moments continue to occur on an everyday basis as I practice these three beliefs. Just as there are layers of injuries in my heart, there are layers of healings that occur over time. As I continue to practice self-awareness, acceptance, forgiveness and love, God gently washes my heart and restores me to wholeness.

———————

These three powerful beliefs sustain my relationship with God and have helped me find the lost treasure of my heart and soul. I can now give to others from a genuine and abundant inner reservoir of love and trust instead of from a desperate need to control or to avoid my emotions.

Using these beliefs regularly has led to a truly satisfying connection with God. That being said, He remains a multi-dimensional mystery and there is still much about Him that I do not comprehend. I have come to accept that I am not meant to understand it all. If I did, then faith wouldn't be necessary; knowledge would be all that I would need.

My initial approach to faith was through head knowledge as I sought to make sense of spirituality. Eventually, I realized that my grasp of it was limited by the confines of my mind. I took a deeper dive into faith, however, when I released my need for complete understanding and began to trust God as I explored the mysteries of my own heart and soul. With this significant step I have found many perspectives and insights that have answered my longing for unconditional love. Exploring the unfathomable nature of God is a lifelong journey, with innumerable rewards.

As we develop a whole-hearted relationship with God, we receive the treasures of love, joy, peace, patience, kindness, goodness, faithfulness, gentleness, and self-control *(The Fruits of the Spirit, Galatians 4:22)*.

As you begin, or continue your faith journey, I offer you this Centering Prayer to strengthen your relationship with God. May it enrich and bless you always.

Centering Prayer

Dear God, be personal and present with me today.
Be my best friend.

Help me to see how you are guiding
and providing for me.
You lead.

Continue to heal my heart swiftly and silently so
that I can be all that you created me to be.
Make me whole.

Amen.

Discovering Strength in Love and Faith

1. What beliefs center and ground you?

2. What pieces of your faith puzzle are you still searching for?

3. What do you do to take care of yourself?

4. How do you know what you need on any given day?

5. What would it be like to seek a more personal relationship with God?

6. What step towards that relationship feels right for you at this time?

7. In what ways will you celebrate what you find, or have already found?

8. What are the challenges you face in trusting God's guidance?

9. In what ways are you willing to partner with God and let the Spirit guide you?

10. What heart healings have you experienced?

11. What healing of your heart would you like to experience?

12. Where will you go from here?

The End...

which is really the beginning...

Reflection Question Index

Acknowledgments

For much of my life I felt that I had a book inside of me, but it wasn't until returning from a trip to Europe that an inner knowing arose which undeniably resounded 'now is the time to write my story'. I started this endeavor naively, not fully knowing what this journey would entail. I am grateful that God provided just the right people along the way to help bring this venture to completion.

Many of the speakers and authors from The Women of Faith organization have inspired me, and I am glad that I chose to use their annual writing contest to set what would be my first book deadline. Doing so motivated me to retreat to the sanctuary of my Cousin Kathleen's farmette, Windrush, on the Eastern Shore of the Chesapeake Bay, for uninterrupted creative time. Both the contest and the writing retreat transformed a pipe dream into a tangible and very real project. I could not have met that deadline without the dedicated support of my dear friend and editor, Linda Brennan. In hindsight, the manuscript we submitted to the contest was very raw indeed, and was one of hundreds received by Woman of Faith; yet the contest served its purpose in getting the book underway. I thank Kathleen for generously sharing her sanctuary with me, and The Women of Faith organization for being a guiding light of inspiration.

I will be forever grateful for Linda's steadfast commitment to what, in the end, became a three year endeavor. She provided inordinate amounts of patience, grace, and wisdom as we re-worked the material again and again and again. Her high standards, attention to detail, and willingness to learn alongside me helped this book become so much more than I could ever have produced alone. Quite simply, Linda, it wouldn't be here without your efforts. We have been on many adventures together, but perhaps this has been the best of all; it certainly has been the longest lasting! I am grateful that you knew when we needed to add the editorial expertise of your sister, Susan Berry, to the project. I appreciate Susan's faith-based perspective and her skillful review of the manuscript, which greatly improved the overall flow and quality of the material. Thank you, Susan, for the time and effort you dedicated to this important work.

I am thankful to the many people that believed in me when I faltered and didn't believe in myself. This sometimes even came from complete strangers who said they wanted to read the book when it was done. I know God planted these anonymous inspirations along the way to keep me going when I felt discouraged.

There were also key people who consistently believed in me more than I believed in myself. My spirits were lifted more than once by my sons Patrick and Ben, my mother Nancy, my siblings, and by many friends and clients too numerous to name. In addition, I felt inspired by my beloved Uncle

Don and the legacy he left behind. I learned from him that some of our most important and lasting work can begin in mid-life. My spirit feels the support that he, my father, and others are sending from beyond the veil.

I am grateful for new, expanding circles of love, and especially appreciate how Karen and Justin Leggett have accepted me into their family and share the light and joy of their sons, Parker and Jacob.

The coaching community which surrounds me promotes lifelong learning and evolution into our best selves. I am grateful for the support and inspiration of so many wise men and women. I thank all of my past teachers and guides to greater consciousness. I especially wish to thank my coaches Nick and Kath, as well as the therapists who guided my growth over the past sixteen years; Ted, Pam, and Mary Liz. You journeyed with me through the process of self-discovery and the expression of my life lessons in written form. I humbly thank you for being witnesses to my growth, and steadfast sources of support, encouragement, and guidance.

I wish to thank everyone who read the manuscript in its many forms and provided feedback along the way. There are too many to name, but you know who you are and I am grateful. You helped to make it better with each revision. I also thank the esteemed authors who gave of their time to read and endorse the manuscript. I especially wish to thank Dr. Bruce Birch for his ongoing encouragement and the Rev. Dr. Susan Halse for being my spiritual guide and pastor. The journey was made richer and more meaningful because of each of you.

Beyond writing my story, bringing this project to completion was an endeavor in itself and the universe provided the people I needed to publish it. I am grateful for the experience and persistence of Beth Mende Conny with WriteDirections. Your expert guidance and at times, tough encouragement, were a tremendous help in the last stages of this project. Heather Akers diligently kept me on track, reminding me to set and honor the necessary deadlines to move this project to completion.

I am very appreciative for the artistic talents of Kim Dow, who designed the interior and cover of the book. Kim, your dedication to this project, along with your talented assistant, Jen Tyler, has been professional, patient, and nurturing – a winning combination. Additionally, I thank Jess deLaski for her cover photography and for consistently encouraging me. Wanda Bulkowski Larsen faithfully provided artistic guidance at a crucial point in the process, which I valued and trusted. Thank you, Wanda, Jess, and Kim for being art angels!

The ability of the heart to continue to heal over time is truly amazing. It is with gratitude that I acknowledge the healing and forgiveness this project has provided in my relationship with my former husband, Matt, and with my deceased father, Ed. Through heartfelt conversations with Matt and my siblings, as well as in the actual process of the writing of this book, I have found the love and caring that exist below the painful memories. I cherish these healing conversations and how they have contributed to my overall wellbeing.

I wish to thank all of my coaching clients who trust me as a partner in their growth. Your dedication to your own development inspires me every day. Your willingness to be vulnerable and open as you courageously move closer to, and through, your growing edges touches my heart. I sincerely hope this story blesses you, and others, who are ready to answer the questions that take them deeper into knowing, loving, and accepting themselves for the wonderful treasures that they are. I also, thank you, the reader for your interest and openness to exploring your search for love and faith.

To my sweetheart Greg, I offer my grateful heart. I am so glad you stopped, looked, and listened to the invitation that God sent our way. I love you, and treasure all that you and I are, and are becoming, together.

Finally, I offer my deepest and most heartfelt gratitude to my creator God who is my constant friend, companion, and guide. This book is an answer to the calling You placed upon my heart and soul. May it be the blessing to others that You want it to be. I am forever yours.

About the Author

Carol deLaski is a professional certified coach (PCC), author, and speaker. She has been an entrepreneurial businesswoman for much of her life with over 25 years' experience in the telecommunications industry. Her passion for clear communication and human development led her to create Clear Choices Coaching, where she provides strengths-based leadership training for businesses and individuals.

Carol is a co-founder of Wholistic Woman Retreats™, a nurturing community which offers enriching and supportive events for women-on-the-grow. Having learned the importance of self-care and taking breaks from the hectic pace of life, she now provides such opportunities for other busy women. She believes that whenever we pause to nurture ourselves we are engaging in a retreat. This community offers programs designed to develop the whole person in body, heart, mind, and spirit. Participants grow stronger in self-awareness and self-care, thereby creating deep and genuine connections with themselves and with others.

Carol is a member of the International Coaching Federation (ICF) and has a Bachelor of Science in Education from the University of New Hampshire. She received her coach training from the ICF accredited Institute for Professional Excellence in Coaching (iPEC). She resides in Maryland.

WHAT'S YOUR STORY?

Carol would love to hear from you
Share your stories of being lost and found as well as your experiences with the Centering Prayer. Please write to her at the address below or contact her through her website: **www.caroldelaski.com**.

Carol offers workshops and retreats based on the principles and practices presented in this book. These programs are appropriate for individuals, couples, and professionals who are interested in seeking and/or supporting the journey towards wholeness of body, mind, heart and spirit. If you wish to receive information about these programs please write or call us.

Carol de Laski
Certified Professional Coach

Clear Choices Coaching
301-371-7460
Contact@caroldelaski.com

www.CaroldeLaski.com

Wholistic Woman Retreats™

Retreats happen every time we pause to take care of ourselves and renew our energy... whether it's a solitary cup of tea, lunch with a friend, or attending an event where we learn something new about ourselves or others.

The Wholistic Woman Community provides a safe place to reconnect with yourself and to make new friends. To receive information on these enriching and supportive programs go to www.wholisticwomanretreats.com and join our mailing list or Like us on Facebook.
We would love to hear from you.

www.wholisticwomanretreats.com
info@wholisticwomanretreats.com

27945233R00196

Made in the USA
Charleston, SC
27 March 2014